LIFE
UN
COMPLICATED

OTHER BOOKS BY THIS AUTHOR

The Leap Year (2017)
Four for the Road (2018)

LIFE UN COMPLICATED

Discovering the calm in the chaos

JANE DELAHAY

Providing professional book design and printing services
for indie authors to tell their stories

www.accentia.com.au

First published 2019

Copyright © Jane Delahay, 2019

The moral right of the author has been asserted.

All rights reserved. Without limiting the rights under copyright restricted above, no part of this publication may be reproduced, in any form or by any means (electronic, mechanical, photocopying, recording or otherwise), without the prior written permission of both the copyright owner and the publishing partner of this book.

Typesetting & Prepared for Publication by: Accentia Design
Typeset in 14/16 pt Garamond Premier Pro
Publishing Partner: Accentia Design Pty Ltd for Jane Delahay
Cover illustration: © 2019 by Anna Blatman (www.annablatman.com)
Cover design: Michelle Hessing
Copy editing: Desolie Page
Printed by IngramSpark, Australia

The publishing partner, staff, agents and author are not liable for injuries or damage occasioned to any person as a result of reading or following the information contained in this book.

A Cataloguing-in-Publication record is available from the
National Library of Australia. http://catalogue.nla.gov.au

ISBN: 978-0-6482776-5-1 (Paperback)

*To Jo, my right-hand woman
(who is left handed),
bestie and breakfast buddy...*

this one's for you.

"New beginnings start from chaos"

~ Jane Delahay

The Greatest Treasure

It seemed to me that for a very long time
This life wasn't really mine
Maybe I was switched at birth
This couldn't be what my life was worth

Sunny days and twinkling stars
And the heavenly smell of cut grass
This was my dream as a child
To answer the call of the wild

We grow up and we falter
And our life gets stranger and stranger
Falling from the tower
Was where I lost my armour

Finding peace and harmony
Was worth the grand ceremony
I have turned around to see
That life is as it should be.

~ *Jane Delahay*

Contents

Prologue	i
Does every cloud have a silver lining?	1
A leap of faith	5
I'm awesome	13
The cloud analogy	25
Fairy dust	35
Let it go! (not the Disney version)	51
Ever tried?	69
Down dog	75
An attitude of gratitude	85
Shiny happy people	107
Peace and quiet	115
This way up	121
Just write	131
Where did I park my broomstick?	145
Love actually	155
Balancing act	159
The thief of joy	173
Cheerleaders	177
Embrace the weird (and wonderful you)	183
Call to adventure	189
A recipe for change	195
Sarah's Fruit & Nut Slice	198
Yellow brick road	199
What I believe (and things I am currently obsessed with!)	203
Thank you	207
About the author	211

Prologue

Let's face it—our world can be pretty crazy. I've lived in it for fifty years and what a ride it's been. Whoa! The proverbial roller coaster ride comes to mind; I'm sure you have shared the same ups and downs of life.

So, what do we make of all of this? This thing called life? It's the million dollar question isn't it? I have a few ideas on how we can swap the fast lane for the slow road. A few years back as I sat across the dining room table with friends, doing my usual arm waving and crying in my soup about how busy my life was and how tired I was, he said, "*You need to uncomplicate your life*". I didn't really take much notice to be fair; I was so caught up in my own world that it didn't register with me until a few weeks later. He had a point, a really big one. My life was complicated. And not just a little bit—I was on the highway to heart attack central.

At that time, I had a full time job managing a team of people, I was raising two teenage children, running a household, trying to see my family and friends as much as possible, managing finances and trying to squeeze in some sort of exercise: the list goes on… this life of mine had become the norm, endlessly busy and not spending any time with myself and doing the things that I wanted to do.

I did a lot of things for other people. What about little ol' me?

Well, little ol' me got cancer. And that stopped me in my tracks. A big bolt of lightning hit me and I had to make changes in my life, big ones. You see, in 2016 my life changed in less time than you can click your fingers. One minute I was grooving along on life's path, and the next minute I was wondering if I would ever see my children grow up. To say it was a shock to be diagnosed with breast cancer would be an understatement, my life fell apart and I didn't know how to fix it. I was lost, confused, scared, and most of all, I hated my life. But I knew deep down that there were better ways to live my life than to be angry, sad, fearful and afraid. I just didn't know how.

So, how do we change our life? We can talk about it (a lot), sing about it or even make fervent plans to get ourselves on track, but it takes more than that. It takes patience, belief, confidence, stamina, caffeine and a little bit of luck. I didn't find it easy (I still don't some days) but little by little I came out of the fog that had enveloped me during cancer treatment and I started by making my life uncomplicated.

≈ ≈ ≈

You might be thinking by now, *'that's all great Jane; it seems like you have a few ideas about this but how do you actually change your life? That's a big call. Isn't this all a bit hokey?'* I hear you, you've tried and you're still in the same place, unable to see the wood from the trees. Your life has gotten in the way and to even think about change sends you into a stricken panic. I get it, I totally do. For a long time I thought that I would just have to deal with the hand I had been dealt, this was my penance of sorts, it was bad luck, and maybe I deserved it? And maybe not. But I had resigned myself to the fact that this was my lot, my life was shizzle and I hoped like crazy that things wouldn't get any worse. I was shouting at the universe that enough was enough; I really couldn't take any more.

There was sunshine on some days but the dark days were more frequent and I thought it would never end, that I would never be the same person again. My whole life had changed in less than a few minutes, I thought that I would have to suffer—like that was the point—maybe I was supposed to suffer? Life as I knew it had ceased to exist and now it was a fight, a fight for my life. During this time, I had a lot of questions about why it had happened to me—I couldn't get past that at the time—I was 'woe is me' for most of my daylight hours. And I was angry.

Coming to terms with the loss of control in my life was hard, harder than I ever thought. This is what made me lost more than anything. I had been the type of person who had control of my life (or so I thought). I feel unbalanced when I can't control the situations I am in. Handing over control to specialists and medical teams was so far from my previous reality that I struggled big time with the enormity of not only my diagnosis but of the impending treatment. I was not a good patient, far from it. I am embarrassed to say that I was a bit rude and a smart arse at some appointments. Something took over me, I could barely control it, my defence mechanisms I suspect. Who were these people telling me what to do? I hated everything to do with it and I could feel the anxiety rising up in me like a volcano, I felt sick to the stomach and I was becoming angrier with every appointment. I remember thinking that none of these people took me seriously and I was just another person in a long line of cancer patients.

How I processed my suffering and distress at the time of my diagnosis was the only way I knew how. My life has been, like everyone else's, a series of experiences that were good, bad or ugly and up until then, had largely been shaped by my parents and my environment. How I reacted was probably a by-product of how I had seen people around me deal with crises and traumatic events. When I look back on major times in my adult life, I came to the conclusion that there were consistently two outcomes: hysteria and indignation. Trauma wasn't a common event in my early life, far from it, but unbeknownst to me, I had subconsciously gathered up this intel in preparation for having to deal with a life-changing event of my own.

And I took the indignation route. I bottled it up and I was resentful, angry and sometimes rather offensive. I can only imagine what some of the people thought of me when I was going through cancer treatment; 'what a bitch' comes to mind.

This is when I started to look at myself. I really wasn't that person, I knew I wasn't. My life was a series of only my own experiences and I knew deep down that no matter how all of these life events had shaped me, I was becoming a rather awful human being. I had built up a wall around myself and I didn't want to let anyone in, my deep rooted sense of unfairness had transformed me into a bitter, self-absorbed and anxiety-ridden person.

≈ ≈ ≈

I had the chance right there and then to change my life. I had the power to attribute meaning to all that existed in my life. I had the power to dictate the effects that this event would have on my life. I was in control.

I started asking myself how these events could serve me and what lessons I could learn from it. It takes some soul searching at best to recognise that you are in control of how you live your life. If you are anything like me, you're puddling along every day hoping and praying that things will change or get better in some aspect of your life. When it doesn't you shrug your shoulders and say 'Oh well, maybe tomorrow'. Well tomorrow comes and goes and before you know it you're approaching a milestone birthday and nothing has changed, in fact it has got worse. You lie in bed at night dreaming of a life that you want, picturing yourself with the things you desire, but you get up the next day and do the same old things over and over again, and again, and again. It's like groundhog day and you realise that unless you give yourself a major kick up the bum, nothing will change and another twenty years will pass and you will be exactly where you are today. For me that was a depressing thought, that I would never realise my dreams and that this was it.

Life had passed me by.

Gosh, there had to more than this, surely?

≈ ≈ ≈

Perspective is a great word. It's not about what you're looking at but where you are looking at it from. Everyone has a different perspective and no two people will see the same things. Every traumatic event in people's lives will be seen differently, thought of differently, processed differently and each person will take something different from the experience. Your experience will never be the same as someone else's, no matter how you look at it: your experience cannot be replicated by anyone else. And this is what makes it hard, not only for you but the people around you.

They don't understand—how could they? It didn't happen to them.

Your approach to your own life is the only way to make change. Even though my beliefs, values and opinions have been largely set from childhood, I realised that I had to change my perspective. *And that is what worked for me.*

Perspective is a point of view or a frame of reference to look at your own life. You need to be willing to change: although we are defined by our experiences, we need to see past them to change.

When you let go of your pre-set notion of your own life, you start to see that there is another way. You can change your point of view, which is why I believe that changing your mind state is the only way to implement real change.

I had to let go of any preconceived ideas about a lot of things. It was like starting at ground zero again, everything that I had gathered up in my brain over the years was useful but it wasn't helping me cope with the emotional fallout from dealing with cancer treatment.

To look at my life differently took courage and to find that place in my heart to allow compassion was the only way I was going to be able to deal with any future roller coaster rides.

Life isn't always black and white, it sometimes doesn't make sense, but this was my life and no matter what it was throwing at me, I was determined not to tumble down the rabbit hole. I picked myself up, dusted myself off and thought, '*If life is gonna give me lemons, I'm gonna make lemonade*'.

And that is what I've done. Making this decision has given me a chance to accept the things I can't change, to find solace in myself and to take life by the reins.

I understand now that life is as one, there are no gaps, I am exactly where I should be. My life is not *happening to me*, it is happening *for me*. And that sense of meaning and fulfilment is really what it's all about.

I have turned my trauma into opportunity, opportunity to change and discovered a new perspective on life. I now see my life through different coloured glasses... and quite frankly I am starting to like the view!

So, does this whole 'change your life' thing work?
Well, it's all in your perspective. If you are prepared to look at things differently, you can change the view.

"Many people have ideas on how others should change; few people have ideas on how they should change."

Leo Tolstoy

INTRODUCTION
Does every Cloud have a silver Lining?

No one really talks about life after cancer or any other traumatic event. In fact, learning to live well after a wake-up call is not well documented (I couldn't find much at the time). I think as a cancer survivor particularly, we should be proud of ourselves for what we have been through. Goodness… most people who have been down this road deserve a medal, a commendation and a lifetime's supply of chocolate. But to tell you the truth, you are thrown to the kerbside of the treatment train and expected to fend for yourself.

The fallout of cancer treatment affects us all differently, for me it wasn't so much the physical side (although at times that was shizzle) it was the domino effect on my mental health.

Survival rates for cancer have soared in the past forty years and whilst this is awesome (I am alive today because of the tireless work of scientists and researchers, thank you) the flipside to this is that, although more people are surviving cancer, there doesn't seem to be the same amount of research dedicated to living well after a diagnosis.

The aftermath of treatment was a minefield for me, my anxiety was sky high and the trauma of what I had been through was hard to comprehend, let alone the emotional shock that was to follow. Navigating my life after cancer became my number one priority, and if I was going to change my own life, then I had a lot of work to do. And that meant I had to do it myself.

There's no manual about how to live life after cancer and even if there was it is not a one size fits all proposition. It's funny now I look back because there is a plethora of material, literature, books and even workshops on how to navigate cancer treatment and all its side effects, so why all of a sudden once you are out the other side, there is nothing?

This got me thinking... I wanted a no-nonsense, common-sense approach to take control of my life, one that was easy to incorporate into my every day. I wasn't interested in anything that was difficult to understand or needed me to make significant change to my daily routines—including any diet that excludes cheese, olives or alcohol. I am, after all, still a mum, wife, daughter, friend, taxi driver for my children and so on. So it was imperative to me to find ways of coping with life changes that fitted into some sort of normal template. So, I have in the last couple of years gathered up a whole lotta stuff about living well and embracing a positive life. And that means all things, including my cancer diagnosis.

This book is about life, and what to do when it throws you a curve ball or two; it's my take on some familiar topics and some not so familiar. They may not suit everyone, you might think they are a bit woo woo, or be totally on board like I am. I don't expect everyone to think that what I write about here is for them, of course not, and that's the best thing about being human—we are all different. I am not sprouting anything here that I don't actually do: I really dislike that. If I'm telling stories then I want them to be honest and not sugar coated. Change is scary and I want to tell you about how I navigated a pretty tough time in my life, not that life is all sunshine and roses, because life isn't like that. Some days I wake up with all the energy and enthusiasm of someone half my age only to find by lunchtime that I feel like someone double my age. Life's like that, it's unrealistic to think that everything you do is going to be successful, exciting or joyful. Life is also mundane, boring and painful... and that is totally OK.

Every chapter in my book is dedicated to something that I now adopt in my everyday life. Some are easy to do, some needed work on my part. I was committed to making real change: in fact most of what I write about is pretty simple to incorporate, you just need the right mind state. I know we don't all have the luxury of free time (me included) but I guarantee you that I have found some of the best ways to incorporate well-being into everyday life. You can do most of the things I talk about in your lunch break, your daily commute, walking your dog or even when you are in the shower.

I didn't attend university to study what I write about here, but I believe that I have graduated from the university of life: these are my truths and my realities.

Hindsight is a wonderful thing, and now that I've had the luxury of several years' reflection, if I can be certain of one thing, it's this: to transform your life you need to change only one thing—*your mind state*. I think that is the real answer. When I reflect back, that was the one thing that made the biggest difference; in fact it is the only thing. When my mind state started to change I saw my world differently, all that had gone before me was irrelevant—it hadn't worked for me anyway. I was open to looking at things differently, I wanted to, I was determined and I wasn't going down without a fight. I was a tough opponent, I gave up many times, I failed, I cried, I sometimes had one too many sauvignon blancs, but I kept fighting. I had so much to live for and I knew that at some stage my life would get better... and it did.

I don't know everything of course, but what I do know is that my world has been opened up and I see things now that give me so much joy that I cannot even believe that I spent years not noticing them. It's often the simplest things in life that give me such delight. I have opened my eyes and my ears to them and they alone have made the biggest impact on my life. Now, I laugh so much more (mainly at myself), stop and smell the roses and realise that my gift is the riches of happiness in living each day with joy.

I know it's clichéd but life is short, this is not a dress rehearsal. Life is awesome, extraordinary, scary and full of the most amazing potential. I am looking forward to finding out what my future holds.

Along the way I have included a few exercises, just in case you are not sure where to start. They're pretty simple and I used them myself to begin with. I also share a few stories from my own life which I hope you enjoy.

Big Love.

Jane x

A Leap of Faith

It is often said that we should follow our hearts, do what we love and the rest will come. But how do you follow your inner most desires, dreams and passions? Somehow we don't really believe we can.

This is a tough one, we all dream about what we would do if we didn't have a mortgage, bills to pay, responsibilities, raising children etc. I had for years thought that to be successful, I had to be working all gods' hours, attending endless events and get-togethers, and running around like a blue arsed fly doing a million things that were nowhere near following my bliss at all. In fact, all I did was run myself into the ground.

If I was going to make a difference in my life and completely change the way I was living then I needed to take a cold hard look at myself. I had worked in a corporate job for nearly twenty years, and most recently in a management position that paid well and provided the lifestyle that I had become totally accustomed to. It was tough going in the early days when I was a new mum; I returned to work a year after my first daughter was born because we needed the money. After my second daughter, I returned three months later, again because we needed the money. Navigating my career and children was challenging, and I was totally sucked into the notion that I could 'do it all'. (I call bullshit on that one). There seems to be this unspoken rule that we're supposed to follow a formula for life after turning eighteen: go to university, get married, buy a house, have children and get yourself into enormous debt to buy things that you don't need.

It was a balancing act between my husband and me to have the children looked after while we slogged away at our jobs that for most part were not the jobs of our dreams. So how do you follow your bliss when you are trapped in this success-driven merry go round? Well, most of us don't, because it's too scary. We don't like change and we certainly don't like poverty.

I used to lie in bed and dream about what I would do if money were no object. I thought about it regularly: if I made more money I could spend more time with my children; if I had more money I could buy a bigger house; if I had more money I could buy a bigger car etc., etc. Money controlled my thoughts, and all I could think about was that if I had more of it, life would be better. It seems crazy to me now because that's totally not what it's all about. Not even close. Even if I had a million dollars in the bank, nothing would change unless I did, and that comes from within. Money is nice, for sure, you can do a lot with it, but it isn't the key to happiness. It was never going to be the key to my happiness. Funny what life throws at us? I was most certainly sleepwalking through my life, going through the motions and hoping at some point that miraculously I would win the lottery or a long lost aunt would leave me her entire estate. What did happen was that I got sick. There's nothing like a cancer diagnosis to put things into perspective. And money had nothing to do with it. No amount of money was going to protect me; money was useless.

To say I reassessed my life would be an understatement. If I was going to survive, I needed to examine everything in my life and put myself first, my well-being was paramount. This got me thinking (a lot) about my real passion, what made me feel alive, happy and fulfilled. I broke it down into parts and listed the things that I loved. In no particular order they are writing, travelling, helping other people, teaching, reading, flowers, animals and yoga. How could I use all these passions, interests and skills to forge myself a new career? And how on earth was I going to do it? Making the decision to quit my job was hard; to be honest I didn't even think I could. I had worked in fashion for most of my career, I loved it but it was the usual 9 to 5 with extra hours commuting, managing budgets and teams of people, and working for someone else. I didn't hate my job but I started to wonder what else was out there for me. Could I really do something else? I was 49 years old, I had a secure job, I was paid good money, isn't that enough? Am I being greedy and self-absorbed to want more from my life?

For years I really knew nothing different, the office was like my second home and I loved the people I worked with. If I left I wouldn't see them every day and I wouldn't have an income to support my family and my lifestyle. Yikes, it was a big decision to go from fully employed to fully jobless. How do you change the life that you have known for so long? 'I couldn't possibly do it, that would be crazy', I used to think to myself. As the months went on, I actually started to resent my job. I wanted to live a different life, and I don't mean that I wanted to be a different person, it wasn't that, I wanted my life to be the one that I had dreamt of, the one where I could live life on my own terms. It became so important to me that I should be true to myself, but what did I really want? Who am I?

Asking myself these questions made me cry. I knew that I had another path, I had been given signs before and totally ignored them. I had been sick before and not taken any notice that I needed to change. I finally stood up and listened. The universe has this way of just telling you what you need to do. I'm no spiritual evangelist, but I know that I was being guided to where I was supposed to be. It's not as crazy as you think—has something or someone ever just turned up in your life and you didn't know why?

I have always loved books and reading, so I followed my heart and took pen to paper and quite frankly, I haven't stopped since. I didn't know to begin with that I wanted to write books and blog, I just wrote about how I was feeling at the time. I was confused and frightened about my future and anxious about all of the medical treatment surrounding my breast cancer diagnosis. Something had to change or things were going to get worse. I wrote my first book for myself, it was my therapy and a starting place for me to heal. It might have seemed a bit self-righteous and vain to some people that I was writing about myself but I didn't care, this was my story and if no one wanted to read it, that was OK too. I didn't write it for anyone else.

    I started to redesign my life into the one that I had only dreamt of. It took over twelve months for me to write my book, I had no idea how it was all going to come together, I just did it. I took the chance any time I had, to write and jot down how I was feeling. I was still working full time but because I loved writing so much, I found time to do it; it was not work to me, I was following my heart and it felt right. Once my creative energy had started flowing, I was on a roll and there were no boundaries. Now that was liberating. I had found my path and I was ready to walk it.

    During that time I also started to really think about what else was happening in my life. I had the chance now to rewrite my own future. I had to stop thinking about the past and start thinking about a life that was not only sustainable but one that made me happy.

    These are big questions to ask yourself, and totally scary to begin with. You know no different and we've been taught not to upset the apple cart. Whether we like it or not, we conform to the ideal that we should have this 'perfect' life and when we don't, we feel like we have failed.

But I was determined that I wanted to change my life and do what I love. I had been preaching the concept that if you do what you love, you won't work a day in your life to my children for years: I needed to start walking the walk and not just talking the talk.

Trusting myself was the first practical step I made. Life challenges are inevitable, but suffering is preventable. Transition is when the big decisions are made. I had to trust and lean into the unknown, no matter how scary that was. Besides, who hasn't made mistakes? We all have. I wanted to live an intentional life from that day forward and live my own story. As far as I was concerned, it was game on.

I woke up one morning and my decision was made, it seemed that the sleep fairies had planted the seed but I had to start watering the thoughts and take action. I didn't consult anyone, not even my husband (I knew that he would start hyperventilating, which he in fact did) but I needed to do this for myself.

I left my corporate job at the end of 2018 to pursue my dream of being a full time writer. Yikes! Talk about a leap of faith. I cannot believe I had done it. Five days before Christmas I said goodbye to my full time management job that I had held for nearly thirteen years. It was a pretty bold move, and to say that I wasn't a tiny bit scared would be an understatement. I couldn't delay it any longer. If turning fifty has taught me anything, it's that you are never too old and it is never too late.

Putting that into practice of course wasn't easy. I had to make some tough decisions and who will ever know if they are the right ones, but hey, I am going to give it a red hot crack. Finding myself sitting at that same desk when I turned sixty was a worse thought than having no job, no money and no career.

≈ ≈ ≈

"Fortune favours the brave."

I'm sure you have heard that phrase. I like it and I don't like it. To be brave can mean so many things: for some, it's brave to catch a huntsman spider in the bathroom and return it to the garden; to others, it's brave to jump out of an airplane. But is it brave to change your life and totally turn your career on its head?

I never considered myself brave but to me brave means heroic, that you have faced unimaginable horror, like war or that you learnt to walk again after crushing your leg. Many people said to me "You are so brave Jane", and while their sentiments were admirable, I never wanted to be seen as brave. I was just getting through my challenges as best I could and I knew many people who had faced bigger challenges than mine. So why do we think that we couldn't possibly be brave? If other people see it in us, why don't see it in ourselves?

Being creative and living a creative life is for the courageous, I know that now. To follow this path is brave; so many have walked it before me, they are my inspiration to keep going and never stop writing. I know it sounds clichéd but I write because I love it, no other reason. If I make a living from it, then that's a bonus. I have to pinch myself every day because I have finally found what I love doing.

Given what I have been through these past few years, I am more than grateful for the opportunity to be sitting here writing for myself and for you. I'm actually super excited about my new creative life. It brings with it so much promise of new beginnings, of living life right now and following my dreams. It's never too late to tap into a creative life, whatever that may be.

When you decide to follow your bliss, it doesn't matter what stage of life you're at when you start. When we follow our hearts everything just seems right, the sun is shining, the birds are singing and all is wonderful in the world. We are constantly smiling and life, my friends, is grand.

As I welcomed in 2019, it was not lost on me how amazing these past few years have been for me. My life has been turned upside down and I love it!

I'm Awesome

I could list here a thousand reasons why I was afraid to change my life, we all have those inner voices telling us that we aren't good enough, or (in my case) that your ideas are unworthy and that no one would read a book you wrote, or that you're too old to change, too young to change, too tall, too short, too fat, too skinny, the list goes on… It is scary and for most of us, believing in ourselves is a luxury we don't allow ourselves to have.

The advice to listen and look to yourself might sound pretty basic, but we aren't very good at looking to ourselves. Why? We don't love ourselves enough.

We human beings are miraculous in every way; quite frankly we should be doing a happy dance every day because it's so awesome to be alive. Hola! but we don't. Instead we hold onto the past, we're cranky pants, angry ants and we turn things over and over in our minds until we make ourselves sick. We are burnt out, exhausted and fearful. It's almost like it bothers us to be here on planet Earth. Sound familiar? Well this was me too (and I thought I could never write a book).

The most important relationship you will ever have is with yourself. When I first heard the phrase '*love yourself*', I thought 'What a load of shizzle'.

I thought the concept of loving yourself was vain and a bit self-important really. But I now know that if we don't love ourselves we cannot transform our lives into the one we deserve.

You see, loving ourselves is about choice. It is the choice to be happy, positive, grateful and kind to ourselves every moment of the day. We either love ourselves or we destroy ourselves, it's really that simple.

The concept of loving yourself is something very foreign to most people, we are not brought up that way in Australia and I suspect there are communities all over the world that don't encourage you to look inward either.

When I was younger, all I saw were the faults, the negative, the 'wish I had', 'wish I was' etc. This view of myself was years' worth of thinking that I didn't quite measure up. When I stood amongst the crowd, I was different (like we all are). I am taller than average, have long (and rather unruly) red hair, freckles, pale skin and abnormally large feet. I felt out of place in my teenage years and whilst I wasn't bullied at school, I do remember overhearing kids call me Carrot Head and Ranga (short for orangutan, if you don't know). I was truthfully an ugly duckling of sorts.

I remember a friend once saying to me in the pale glow of a street lamp, "You are quite pretty in this light". Talk about not feeling that great about yourself, to me that translated as I was only pretty in the dark. Super I thought, I will just live my life at night-time like a vampire.

As I grew into my twenties and away from the pack mentality of the school yard, I blossomed. I got married, bought a house and started travelling. I had always had a keen and intellectual mind, and during this time I had got myself a proper job and was living life, making memories and having fun.

It wasn't until my forties that the wheels started to fall off.

I wasn't young any more, the sparkle in my eyes had faded and I felt that people only saw me as a mum, and not the person I was before having children. I started to think, 'Is this it? Is this all there is?' My self-esteem was bottoming out and I felt invisible.

I did a few crazy things in my early forties to try and regain my youth but all that ended up doing was making me feel diabolically hungover on a Saturday morning. I couldn't sustain it anyway and quite frankly I was just being ridiculous hanging out with people who were ten years younger than me.

What a wakeup call.

I was lost and I didn't know where to turn; was I actually having a mid-life crisis? Who even knows what that is supposed to feel like? I just felt old and sad. I didn't look at myself much then, only to brush my teeth and even then it was a fleeting glance in the mirror. I was rolling along, wayward and with no real direction. Not once did I think that I needed to look inward; that sort of practice belonged to a world orbiting in another planet. Not on my watch.

The next few years were pretty unremarkable and I plodded along living a very unaware life. I never saw the world happening around me, I was self-critical, self-absorbed, a gossip and I complained about everyone around me.

I now call this my 'life confusion stage'. Who was I? I had no purpose, no real purpose, nothing that made me leap out of bed every morning and inspire me to be the best version of myself. I was in fact trapped in my own life, thinking that fulfilment was about material things and not the value of life.

I have since found out that this is not uncommon in this stage of people's lives. They (like me) have been focusing on raising children and building a home life of security, success and wealth. This is what we think we are supposed to do. Our society seems to have these rules around what is deemed to be successful. I bought into that too: I wanted the nice house, fancy car and overseas holidays too.

In my view, this notion of 'success' is muddled—it's taken me a long time and an illness to get this—but for years all I did was plunge myself headlong into a stressful and demanding life. Working to the point of exhaustion, being (so called) busy and being seen at the office until all hours is deemed to be the pinnacle of success—who even thinks that this is sustainable? It's not, unless you want to drive yourself into an early grave. And that wasn't very appealing.

I had got to my mid-forties and I was exhausted,

I had achieved a lot in that time, but at what expense?

It's no wonder I got sick, I was on a one-way road to stress city and I didn't even know it. I thought my duty was to look after my children, my family and, if I had anything left in the tank then I would do something for myself. This order isn't right, how could I teach my children about self-love if I put myself last all the time?

When I reflect on that time I try not to feel sad, because I really didn't know any better. I never knew that there was a whole world out there that could bring sense and meaning to my life. And it wasn't what I thought it was. It certainly wasn't money. It was about making sense of the essence of myself and staying connected to the person that I was born to be. I know, whoa!, it sounds all evangelistic but what a revelation.

Even writing this now makes me wonder how on earth I got on in life for all those years without spending any time with myself. Geez, what was I thinking?

It wasn't easy at first to realise that the universe was telling me something. I was angry, sad, scared and fed up with life when I was diagnosed with breast cancer. I definitely didn't feel very awesome then, I can tell you! The shift took time and dedication on my part. It didn't happen overnight that's for sure, it was a very gradual process for me to fall in love with myself again. That wonderful person that lived inside me was begging to get out. I had to let the sunshine in.

I started to read a lot, mainly about depression—cue my love of Ruby Wax's books, *Sane New World* and *Frazzled*. She has a way with words that really resonated with me at the time and I love the fact that she takes the piss out of herself.

One of Ruby's first chapters in Sane New World is titled '*What's wrong with us?*' She explains that we humans are constantly beating ourselves up and competing with ourselves, and that it's no wonder we are burnt out, stressed and depressed (along with many other things). She explains that we are either evolving or dissolving and we need to maintain our individuality because no one will do it for us.

Ruby takes us through her own journey and in the end we have a list of tools that can help us understand ourselves and why we do the things we do. My take on this is that we need to look inward, not outward; forget what society says about what is successful. Make your own rules and start thinking about how you can connect with yourself. Life isn't unfair (contrary to popular belief), we need to reward ourselves and learn greater wisdom.

We all know that we are one of a kind; the things that make us all different are the things that we need to embrace (even abnormally large feet).

We hear all the time that there is no such thing as normal, and there isn't.

Your normal is you.

There is no one comprehensive way to live, or a normal way to look or even feel.

You are an authentic 'once-only, one-off'.

Pay attention to your life, because it is not waiting.

It isn't always easy or comfortable to love yourself, but it's worth it. The old adage, if you don't love yourself, who will?, is truer today than it ever has been.

If you carry your insecurities and lack of awesomeness around like an overweight backpack, you will eventually crumble at the knees and fall flat on your face.

Having the courage to pack a little more lightly will change the weight and allow you to travel with a comfortable amount of appreciation.

Start having a loving relationship with yourself, it's a lifelong romance, as Oscar Wilde would say.

Exercise

Mirror, mirror on the wall...

Stand in front of the mirror and smile at yourself.
I know, this might seem a bit silly to begin with, and you may feel weird, but you can do it. I know you can!

Really take a look at yourself, and by this I mean **REALLY** taking a look at yourself. Look into your eyes, right into the middle of them, stare at yourself for two minutes. Study the shape of your face. What do you see? *Try not to be critical, just look, as if you were looking at yourself for the very first time. Look at you, a perfect human being.*

Spend a minute a day when you are doing anything in front of the mirror and stop to spend time looking at you.

This exercise has so many wonderful benefits from something that is so easy to do. I also say out aloud "I'm awesome!", when I am looking at myself, it is such a lovely thing to say and for you to hear, I encourage you to give it a try. No one need be around when you do this, or you could say it in your mind, whatever way you do it, it's important that we understand that we are in fact pretty awesome.

The first time I did this I cried (I actually still do when I do this exercise) but it is so important to look at ourselves and see what is really there, as we are practically perfect in every way. We truly are.

Think about all the times you have stood in front of the mirror, to do your makeup, brush your teeth, pluck your eyebrows; we see ourselves every day but we don't *see* our real selves. Our eyes deceive us, when we really look, we see things we have never seen before.

On the next few pages, write down some words you would say to yourself when looking in the mirror and what you see.

Words you would say to yourself

The Cloud Analogy

Mind chatter... argggh!, that old chestnut (and one I struggled with big time). The mind is continually gathering information from everywhere, and these days it's more like bombardment. In our smart phone era it's almost impossible to switch off. I read recently that the average smart phone user checks their device 150 times a day! Whoa, no wonder we can't switch off.

I call this inner prattle the 'monkey mind' (I learnt this one from my yoga teacher). Think of a monkey swinging from branch to branch. Is that what your mind is like? Mine was... going from one unhelpful thought to another. *'I can't do this or that'*, *'I'm too tired'*, *'My life is too hard'* and so on.

Chatter, chatter, chatter, every minute of the day—I was always criticising myself. It's a wonder my brain didn't explode. I am not alone in thinking this way; it has become a natural state for many of us.

Studies have shown that the brain detects negative information faster than positive information (what a bummer). Our brains are wired for catastrophe. This would explain why the news is so depressing—have you ever wondered why the top five stories are always bad news? It's because we are intrinsically attracted to it. This is why I have stopped reading, watching or listening to the news. Part of our brain is still operating on the fight or flight responses from millions of years ago when all we had to do was survive. And that meant being on the constant look out for predators (the ones with sharp teeth). That kind of danger doesn't pop up so much in our twenty-first century world, but that inbuilt negativity does some real damage when we turn it on ourselves.

I was the queen of mental chatter. You all know the stats that say we have thousands of thoughts every day and a large proportion of those are thoughts from the previous day, and the previous day... I would churn those old chestnuts around in my mind for days on end and get myself in quite a state, usually to the point that I was a bundle of nerves and bordering on a panic attack.

I would replay scenarios over and over in my mind, generally trying to think of ways that I would change things, seem more intelligent or just to show someone that I was superior. What the?!

I remember endless situations of being in my own private mind nightmare; they would engulf me so that I couldn't think of anything else. It was all consuming and frightening that I let my thoughts rule my inner world.

My poor husband would listen intently as these irrational and absurd thoughts would pour from my mouth in a verbal waterfall. My mind was silently thinking it couldn't take any more chatter and I would unleash my inner world on my husband. This was especially true after my cancer diagnosis. My mind was more than swinging from branch to branch; I was swinging across a ravine, barely hanging on to the rope. I was so caught up in my own private misery that I never stopped once to think about why I felt that way; it was just easier to have my own silent pity party.

I realised it was time to quieten the chatter and noise. I knew I had to, so I started to read (a lot) about mindfulness. I know it's a bit of a buzzword, and there is confusion around what it really is, yet I like to think of it like this:

Think about what you are thinking about.
That's it.
It's OK to have thoughts. We all have them.

Mindfulness means paying attention in the current moment. There is no judgment about what you're thinking about, it's just a thought. Think about where your thoughts came from in the first place? Your parents? Your teachers? Your sisters or brothers? Most of us are unaware of how we came to the thought processes we inhabit. These thought patterns of ours are old; they form when we are very young and we carry them into adult life and then they don't go away until we recognise them and change their radio frequency.

Thinking about what we are thinking about is unnatural to most of us, and certainly was for me. I never recognised what I was thinking about for 90% of the time, and the other 10% was usually negative. I must say when I first staring looking into this practice of mindfulness, I was puzzled. How do you even listen to your thoughts? What are you supposed to do? Do I need a special pair of earphones for that?

I like the analogy that thoughts come and go like clouds. Some days it was pretty windy in my head, those clouds were whirring past, the constant berating exhausting me. Yet for the most part I started to recognise them, examine them and then let them go on their merry way.

If they came back, I would say "Hey, I've heard you before", accept it and then move on to the next thought. That's not to say that what was going on between my ears was always positive, it wasn't—still isn't!—but I was certainly becoming aware of them.

That is the hardest part of starting this practice, getting on top of those menacing thoughts that you know are detrimental to you but you just can't stop! It's like the chocolate bar you open and say *"I'll only have four squares"* and then find ten minutes later that the whole bar is gone.

You can't help yourself and before you know it, you're in a screaming heap again.

This happened to me last year when I had a strange uncomfortable pain in my stomach; it felt like I had indigestion all the time. I tried medication, it didn't work and I was certain that I had some awful condition that would send me back down the path of a cancer diagnosis again. My mind was rampant, I couldn't help myself. Even though I could realistically deduce that it probably wasn't cancer, I still thought the worst. I went off and had all the tests and they came back negative. There was nothing wrong with me. In fact the doctor said that I should probably consider some counselling. It was all in my head, I had let something quite minor become all-consuming and set myself off on the roller coaster of disaster when I should've known better. (I need to read my own book, LOL). But this was a reminder to me that I still have a way to go in this mindfulness game. It isn't something that happens overnight, that is for sure: it takes practice.

I have adopted the cloud analogy into my life and it has worked for me. My mind is still jammed with thoughts but I work at releasing them as best I can, I try to envisage exactly that—clouds passing by, floating away. Nothing else, just letting them float away.

I still have days when I have a familiar feeling in my chest (like an elephant is sitting in there) of the sunken negativity that haunts me from time to time.

I am not sure what brings it on, I have tried to connect the dots but my practice of mindfulness has taught me that it is OK to think this way but to recognise the thoughts for what they are—just thoughts.

I have found this practice to be one of the easier ways to immediately change what's going on in my head.

I liken the noise to the dull hum of the television in the background, it's there but you don't have to pay attention.

...and I don't.

Exercise

Changing your thinking...

I know this sounds simple, and it is—*on paper*.
I know you're saying:
"*I cannot get that thought out of my mind, it's replaying like an old record*" but I encourage you to not try too hard–trying is an effort.

In this exercise, let the thoughts come and go, but start to gently recognise them.
Break your thoughts down, examine them.
We are our thoughts—*really think about that one.*

Step outside your thoughts and just observe them.
Increase the space between you and your thoughts.
Notice that you are not your thoughts, they are separate from you.
Spend time becoming aware of you and your thoughts.
You can do this whilst doing anything—watching TV, doing the dishes, walking your furry friend—any time of the day.

If you notice that the chatter bugs are creeping in again, just observe. Don't struggle with them; let them come up and out.
Feel your feelings.

We become what we think about. When we are thinking about negative things all the time, that is what comes true for us. If you say to yourself "*I'm fat*", "*I'm old*", or "*I'm unlovable*" and so on... that is your thought pattern and, by default, your life will be the same.

Try changing the voice inside your head to "*I am worthy of love*", "*I have a womanly shape*", "*I am mature and wise*".

Turn the words around to the positive... and mean it.

Whenever I feel a bit shizzle, I say:
I am happy.
I am healthy.
I am wealthy.

Whenever we say "*I am*" instead of "I should be" or "I could be", we turn the attention to ourselves. It's a simple thing to do–become more aware of how you talk to yourself. Change it up and see how you feel. I'm guaranteeing you will feel a whole lot better!

Once you start to recognise your thoughts, you give the negative ones less attention and they stop replaying over and over. (That's not say that they may not crop again the next day, but you will know what they are and then you can use the cloud analogy).

These thoughts may be true to you right now, or you may feel that they are, but they can be changed.

All thoughts can be changed.

Fairy dust

Remember when you were a child? When life was full of excitement and wonder? Practically everything was magical.

What were your dreams when you were a child? Did you want to fly a plane, build houses, take photographs, play music or be a parent?

I wanted to write stories. But, somehow in between the innocent wonder of my dreams to facing the reality of the grown up world, my dreams faded; I had all but given up on living the life of my dreams. I was embarrassed to dream and feared that people would see them as silly and trivial. Adults don't have dreams; they say, "You couldn't possibility have a dream?" Pfft I say!

Most of us now live on broken dreams, ones that were vivid and strong once upon a time, but not now. We grow up and we forget what we dreamed of. When we were children we were full of excitement for even the smallest of things, dragonflies in the garden, daisy chains, shiny shoes and leaves falling from trees. In our naive child's mind there were fairies in the garden, angels in the sky and ruby slippers. I had all but forgotten about this in my day-to-day adulting life. It's one of the most wonderful feelings to be hypnotised by sheer delight, it gives us a spring in our step and a feeling that everything is good in the world. I wanted to feel like that again.

My early childhood was often spent with a family friend of my mum's. They lived in a country town smaller than where we lived in the eastern part of Victoria; I'm told less than 400 people lived there. It was (and still is) an attractive town with a pleasant rural atmosphere, where people don't lock their houses or cars, everyone knows each other's families and the locals are proud of their history. It has managed to hold onto its significant small town charms and boasts wide open spaces, community gardens, Neighbourhood Watch and Girl Guides. In the summertime, our friend's garden was perfect, a tall magnolia tree stood handsomely as the centrepiece emitting that glorious scent that only comes from the warm, humid, summer air. I remember the scene like it was yesterday, smiling faces, incessant chatter, and children running around the legs of the adults, and swinging on the ropes strung between two large tree boughs at the back of the garden. It was magical, I loved this garden. It was the most perfect place. Full of hidey holes for small children to look for garden fairies, cool patches of heavenly violets to sit and read, big fat leaf canopies to shade you from the sun and the most enchanting higgledy piggledy tree house sprouting up from the very back corner of the garden. It was a child's perfect place, like transporting yourself into the splendid world of the magic garden.

Our friend was a primary school teacher and, not surprisingly, she had an enormous amount of books, all different types of picture books, novels and classics. I loved them all, I suspect my devotion to books started around this time too. I couldn't wait to see what new ones had appeared since I was last there. I have since spoken to my mum about all the beautiful books I remember and she said she cannot recall them—funny, isn't it, what you recollect? I was so engrossed in the world of books, I noticed them everywhere.

I recently spoke to a friend who is an avid reader just like me and she said that neither of her children read, especially not just for the pleasure of it.

I have always immersed myself in books; Enid Blyton was my favourite author as a child. I truly believed there was a Faraway Tree with magical folk. I loved reading about Moonface, Silky and the Saucepan Man. I could escape into that world whenever I wanted. I had a love for the world of books and my imagination ran wild. I believed in Santa Claus, the tooth fairy, unicorns and animals that could talk. They may have been my beliefs from reading fairy tales but how utterly delightful it was to be part of such a magical world, even if it was inside my head. I desperately wanted to visit the folk in that magical tree and live their adventures. I still do!

I often reflect on these childhood memories, as one does when you have children of your own.

What is it that makes you reminisce and feel fuzzy? It's the magic of it all, the simplicity of that time of your life, just enjoying being a child and knowing that life was wonderful; you didn't know anything else really.

≈ ≈ ≈

My mum's friend is of Dutch descent, and they always celebrated Christmas on the 24th December. It was a big deal. At the end of the night when we were making our way home from the festivities in that state of half sleep, we would step out in to the summertime air and look up at the stars. "If you look really close you can see Santa and his sleigh coming", my parents would say... and I totally believed them. It has taken many years for me to come back to that place of belief and I wonder how I could possibly have let it go.

Believing in something magical is delightful. As I've been known to say, "To believe in magic is to believe in yourself". I love that, it sums it all up really. Life is supposed to be magical.

We have all been given a gift but somehow we succumb to living a life of drudgery, slogging away at jobs we hate and thinking that is all this world has in store for us. To transport ourselves back to the time when life was full of marvellous things and nothing seemed impossible is akin to getting ourselves checked into the funny farm. No one thinks that you should feel that way as an adult. But I actually think that it is grown-ups that have it all wrong: to be disenchanted by life and all its wonder is one of the most depressing things I hear and see in my day-to-day life.

When people talk about their dreams or a job they would love to do, a smile instantly lights up their face, they are excited to be even thinking about it and how if they could possibly do something as fantastic as that, they would be on cloud nine. Giving ourselves permission to live the life of our dreams is about breaking the rules—we need to step up and out of the confines of what society says we can and cannot do.

This is a foreign concept to most people. You don't hear people in conversation saying "Hey, I just wrote a list of my dreams, want to hear what they are?" Unlikely, because no one thinks that their dreams can come true. I didn't grow up in an especially creative or dream-centred family. That's not say that my parents weren't ambitious, they were, we had a lovely home, we were educated and we didn't go without anything we really needed. This notion of believing in yourself and your dreams was brought to my attention recently after talking to my mum. Let me tell you her story.

She has in the past two years starting singing again. My mum had not sung in a choir (or anywhere else other than the shower) for fifty years. Yes, fifty years. That's how long it had taken her to realise that the something missing in her life was her love of singing. As a teenager she had sung in the school choir and loved it, it was her passion, her outlet and her own creative joy. It took only one teacher (or choir mistress, I'm not sure) to tell her that she at best was pretty average.

This discouraged my mum and she never went back. It seemed that there was no place for someone like her who just wanted to enjoy the simple pleasure of singing, regardless of whether she was good at it or not.

Fast forward fifty years and my mum is singing her heart out. She was nervous to be even thinking about the prospect of singing again. She was after all nearly seventy years old and faced the likelihood that she would be singing with people half her age, and with a lot more experience. But that didn't discourage her. She knew that this was something that she had to do; it was what she loved, like her inner child was telling her that it's OK now, you are safe, and you can pursue your dream. She didn't want that to pass her by again, to miss the wonder of living her dream. She had let her dream of being a singer go and now it was time to grab the reins again.

She now has professional singing lessons and is part of two choirs that regularly perform at retirement villages, local churches and their own annual shows. She has even done a few solos, and is improving her skills every week. Her repertoire is extensive and she regularly breaks into song whenever she feels the urge to sing (which is often).

So what does this tell you? That following your dreams is not always about a career or making money. I don't think it's ever about that, it's about pursuing something that makes your heart sing (literally). We all know that feeling that comes when we do something that brings us utter joy, it's a great feeling and our world makes sense to us. It's like life on steroids, it's big and brash and full of wonder. And I think my mum is pretty awesome for never giving up on her dream, even if it took fifty years.

≈ ≈ ≈

Three years ago I wrote a list of my dreams (it was long): I wanted to be a published author, travel overseas, buy a new car, have my health back and be a writer full time. Yikes, at the time I thought that I had indeed gone to crazy town. But here's the thing (apart from a new car) I did it.
It was now or never,
I had to decide what was important to me, the real me.
Not what I thought someone else thought was right for me—how could they even know anyway!

I started by making a list of what I really wanted in my life.
It didn't matter whether they were achievable or not, that's the point of writing your dreams, big things, or little things, it doesn't matter. It is so much fun (I'm pretty sure that I put on my list that I wanted to cultivate orchids, didn't do that one, but hey, I've still got time!)
I also wrote down where I wanted to travel, people I wanted to meet, places I wanted to visit and things I wanted to do. I transported myself back to the time in my life when there were no boundaries; if I could dream it, then I could actually do it. And here's the thing, you need no-one's permission to do it.
We all have the ability to do what sets our hearts on fire. We all have the ability to enjoy doing something meaningful for ourselves and others. We should live our lives to their full potential and believe we are capable of doing anything we dream of. We tell our children that, but unless we are living examples, they fall into the

same trap we did.

If you are alive, then you are capable of living the life of your dreams, and even if for some of the time you think that you're not capable, at least give it a red hot crack.

So, my message today is, go after your dreams, catch them, or you will never realise them.

Enliven yourself and give yourself permission to listen to your own voice, celebrate your mistakes, acknowledge them and then create your very own fairy dust.

Exercise

Catching your Dreams...

For this exercise you will need to grab a piece of paper or your computer or write on the following pages, and make a list of what you really want in your life.

These can be big things, or little things, it doesn't matter. This can be (in no particular order):
Relationships
Career
Money
Health
Family
Personal.

**Think about what you really want, be quite specific about the kind of career (for instance) you want.
What would it be?
What do you love doing?
What is important to you in your dream job?
How does it look?**

See these things in your mind's eye, see yourself doing them.
Be as bold as you like, this is your list of dreams, just go for it!

_____

_____

_____

_____

Once you have written down your dreams they become more powerful—it's there in black and white. You can add to them anytime, keep your list going.

I am also a fan of the mood/vision board (or dream board may be more appropriate here). It can be any size, I put mine above my calendar, so it's about an A4 size but hey, go to town, make it poster size if you like.

You may like to choose a cork board, a bright piece of cardboard or a fabric board, it doesn't matter, whatever you fancy!

Fill it with photos, pictures, quotes, anything that will inspire you every day to reach for the stars and start living the life of your dreams.

You may draw you inspiration from travel, beauty, nature, animals, architecture or food (I'm always dreaming of gingerbread).

Having visuals of the things that you desire makes it real. Put it somewhere where you will see it every day, put it on your fridge, your wall above your desk, inside your wardrobe door (maybe not in your sock drawer).

This is also such a fun thing to do, it's like being back at school and cutting up your mum's magazines, all you need is your imagination and a glue stick. You can add to it anytime you like, nothing is set in stone, it's a work in progress, just like you.

Remember that these are your inspirations to keep and work towards you manifesting all the good in your life.

Let it Go!

(not the Disney version)

Without fail every week I have breakfast with my dearest friend Jo. Nothing gets in the way of our weekly catch ups, laughter, caffeine and beach walking (well, sometimes the rain). One Sunday morning Jo was telling me all about her decluttering frenzy. She had made some major inroads into freeing up an amazing amount of space in her wardrobe and she loved it. This got me thinking, our lives are full of stuff that we don't need. Let's be honest here, who really needs that latest whiz-bang gadget?

Stuff complicates things, creates messy minds and creates chaos without us even knowing it. We live in a world that encourages us to have more stuff; we "buy" into the notion that we need all these things to make us happy. We don't. We all have too much stuff, not just material stuff, mental stuff too ('fuzzy head syndrome', I like to call it). Our lives are full of stuff that we don't need. Seriously, we need a lot less than we have to live.

Here's a thought. People now have so much more than they did fifty years ago (a lot more). We should be grateful that we live in such abundant times, but are we? It seems to me that we have so much stuff because we are driven by this notion that success equals money which equals stuff. It's a relentless addiction to be keeping up with the person next door. The constant wanting of material things leaves us in a state of both craving and dissatisfaction. Our minds are conditioned into a state of having or not having. It's an all-consuming merry go round. No level of stuff is going to satisfy this hunger; as we well know (and has been well documented) stuff does not make us happy. It has the opposite effect: our well-being starts going backwards.

In fact in our modern world, we have stuff overload. We are surrounded by stuff; everywhere we go, there is something to buy, something to acquire, or something to possess. Nowadays our society leans more towards consumerism, materialism and a disposable culture. How many times have you heard your parents say, "They don't make 'em like they used to", and they would be right. When something breaks down or falls apart, we don't try and fix it, we toss it away and buy a new one. Stuff isn't designed to be fixed: it's designed to have a short life so it can be replaced, it keeps the wheels of consumerism rolling along, and keeps us buying more and more stuff.

As we travel through life, we inevitably encounter challenges and speed bumps, which is when it is even more important to examine and scrutinise all of the stuff we have gathered. Illness is one of those times but it can also happen when you move house or your children grow up.

Stuff has this power to evoke emotions that you didn't even know were there—funny, isn't it, that we attach so many memories to stuff? This can have its upsides and downsides, holding onto stuff can make us happy or a weeping wreck.

I have seen countless programmes on television and social media about decluttering. My girlfriend Jo is a perpetual declutterer and even puts videos on her Facebook page to encourage other people to do it.

I am a fan of decluttering; there's a real sense of accomplishment when you have finally got around to sorting out the junk drawer. Deciding to downsize and declutter can be a very liberating experience, but for many, the thought of that brings up feelings of dread—and you are not alone.

To be honest I had let this one go when I first got the urge to start reorganising my space junk. I wasn't ready; the thought of sifting through all my stuff was too much for me. I didn't have the mind space for it nor the capacity to "let go" of the stuff that was hiding in the bottom drawers.

It was too overwhelming at the time of my diagnosis and treatment so I had to say to myself, "One thing at a time".

And this too is something that shouldn't go unmentioned.

It is totally OK to get all revved up to do something and then not do it.

I knew that I needed to create some order in my life but I had to wait for the right time. It's an exercise that needs to be done in small chunks. Announcing that you are going to declutter your home and your head in one fell swoop will end in tears. Believe me, I've been there.

Thankfully (with a bit of planning) decluttering can be a really gratifying and cathartic exercise, and I'm glad that I finally started cataloguing and classifying my rather large book collection.

I also bought a shredder. I kid you not; I had paperwork dating back to 1997, boxes and boxes of it. They had been hiding upstairs, out of sight for more than twelve years, I couldn't face it and every year the pile got bigger.

I'm sure you know that sinking feeling every time you walk past something that you know needs your attention but you just can't get started.

It was overwhelming and a mammoth task but once I had gotten over the first hurdle, I was on a mission. I actually killed the first shredder I bought, totally burnt out the motor with the sheer amount of paper I was shredding. My recycling bin was constantly stuffed full of confetti sized shreds that would fly around my neighbourhood for days after bin night. As it happens (which I didn't know) you can only shred for two minutes before you have to 'rest' it.

It took months.

I am happy to say that I am nearly there and my lounge room has returned to its normal condition, not reminiscent of a winter wonderland covered in paper dust.

So, my take is this, tackle one thing at a time. I suggest one drawer or cupboard at a time actually. Set a time once a week for only an hour (that's all, let's not go crazy here). I suggest a weekend day—we're all in a better mood on the weekend.

Exercise

Decluttering...

Start by selecting one drawer.

Tip your drawer out onto the table or floor and have a good look at the contents. Do you really need anything?

Has it got a purpose or is it just that you may need it one day?

Be honest with yourself.

The old adage suggesting that if you haven't used it in the last year, you don't need it rings absolutely true.

Make two piles, one to keep and one to give to charity/friends or the bin. Your Keep pile should be one quarter of the Throw pile.

Decluttering is an awesome thing to do, it instantly makes you feel better. Start by clearing out the old and bringing in the new (just not too much new clutter, ha ha).

In case you were wondering, this is my list of stuff that has now permanently left my house (happily ever after...):

- Socks with holes (or no mates)
- Clothes that don't fit (let's be honest here!)
- Broken coat hangers
- Containers with no matching lids
- My children's drawings from kindergarten (I know, but I had hundreds of them!)
- Anything that had expired, food, medicines, make up, curry powder (the list goes on...)
- Cushions that had gone flat and lumpy
- Broken or chipped pots, plates, mugs and glassware
- Keys that don't fit any lock in my house, car or garage
- Pens that don't work
- Towels that had bleach stains
- That collection of glass jars (I was going to make jam in last winter, and never did)
- Light globes that had blown
- Magazines from 1989 (although looking back at the fashion was extremely funny).

≈ ≈ ≈

There is certainly more to life than stuff, and after I got cracking tackling my own stockpiles I began reading a bit more about living with less clutter.

At the opposite end of the spectrum is the concept we now know as 'hyper frugality'. I am a fan of this too but possibly not in the extreme. I am all for creating experiences above having possessions, but to give away all of my possessions would send me into a spin.

I can understand the attraction of downsizing, especially at my age and the inevitable empty nest, but to totally discard everything I have gathered over the past fifty years would leave me feeling like I had no identity. I guess that is the point of frugality, it's a lifestyle change. I do know of people who have sold up everything, grow their own food, make their own clothes and live practically on the smell of thin air. God knows how they do it. I don't consider myself to have an overabundance of possessions, but to live without my coffee machine would need some serious consideration.

But, there is certainly an appeal to living more frugally, 'less is more' brings a whole new meaning when you're faced with a life changing illness.

It was during this time that I realised that none of this stuff of mine was going to get me through cancer treatment (except maybe my coffee machine). I had worked hard for my possessions but they were exactly that, possessions, I had never even thought about why I needed them and what encouraged me to own them.

Their value was not as meaningful as I thought; I too had been swept up in the belief that if I had these things my life would be better. It made no difference when I was diagnosed; in fact I hated all that junk in my home, it made me panic.

During this time I established what my priorities actually were. Looking for meaning in my stuff wasn't cutting it, so I had to look elsewhere. For my part, I did a lot of inward looking (cue everything I talk about in this book!) but I was also fascinated by the rise of the movements associated with the sharing and experience economies. It's a pretty new concept and I am on board. It essentially means that we value experiences over possessions. It has definitely got some momentum behind it, with politicians and businesses particularly embracing the well-being culture above consumerism. The well-being concept is having its day in the sun and I am very excited about that. The shift in our quality of life, sustainability and happiness has got to be something to look forward to and I like the fact that we can all get on board. This is not something that we just leave to the experts. I already know that I am thinking this way; I value what people do, not what they have, and adopt the same values in my own life.

I spend most of my money on travelling, and for me this is all about experiences. I love the idea that while money can't buy happiness it can buy me a plane ticket, it's pretty much the same thing. To experience the wonder of this planet is for me, a true life experience and whenever I get to share that with my family it's even better. Because no matter where you go, it's your memories that are precious, not whether you ate at a five star restaurant or bought a fancy pair of shoes.

The best experiences are those that cost nothing. When my sister and I travelled to Greece recently, my most favourite time of the day was after dinner when we returned to our room and had a cup of tea together. It was a perfect time of day to sit, relax and talk. I realise now that I am at my happiest when I can experience stuff, not buy it.

≈ ≈ ≈

I think it was Snoopy (from the Peanuts comic strip) who suggested that when you have the courage to let go, being happy becomes your default position.

There are so many things that we need to let go of, past grievances, self-limiting beliefs, self-doubt, lack of confidence, the list goes on, and on...

I know, we all have them (seeing we are all friends here) but I still find it hard to let go of my feelings about my cancer diagnosis. From time to time, I replay in my mind how I would do things differently. Not helpful. There is nothing I can do about what has happened in the past, it's done and dusted. Finished, full stop. So why do we find it so hard to let go?

We seem to be hardwired to hold on to every wrong-doing, injustice and unfairness for the term of our natural lives. I was no exception. Finding room in our minds and hearts is important, we need to clear out the chaos so that we can breathe and have space to flourish and to have the ability to let go of grudges, fear, worry and anything that upsets your apple cart. Creating balance in our lives allows us to live the life we are meant to.

I am a fan of adopting the "tree" method in our lives. Every autumn, trees shed their beautiful leaves, the trees let the leaves go and they fall to the ground. It is nature's cycle to discard what they don't need. Autumn symbolises the need to be changeable and move towards the next season. How perfect. Nature has this wonderful way of spring cleaning and making space for the new by clearing out the old. Take a leaf out of that book (pardon the pun) and shed the leaves that you don't need.

Letting go is tough, we think that if we do, we will lose too much of ourselves. When people think of loss they think of losing something, not gaining something. Loss can mean many different things, by definition it means "come to be without, to be deprived of". For most of us this can sometimes mean small losses like losing our keys or money, your football team losing a game, or losing your job, losing a much adored pet and, worst of all, losing a loved one. Loss is seen mostly as a bad thing, an almost helpless state of grief, loss is scary and it is frightening. We don't know how to process it.

It is basic psychology that we define the term negative as bad and positive as good. But I think that we have that a bit muddled - negative does not always mean bad and positive does not always mean good. By interpreting an event or a situation as negative, we immediately block our minds to it being anything else and it affects our thoughts and behaviour.

I had to shift this mindset: what if the worst day of my life ended up being the best day of my life? I needed to transform my thoughts into something optimistic and affirming, regardless of how I felt about it.

I love the story from the Buddhist teaching of the Sallatha Sutta and the arrow; it is one of my favourite stories. It says that if the arrow hits you, you will feel pain where it struck. This can mean many things that happen in our lives every day, like being sick, being in an accident or your car breaking down, and yes, they cause some pain. But it is the second arrow that we fire that amplifies the pain. It is our own thoughts, feelings and reactions that cause the suffering. Letting go of what makes us sad, angry and fearful is a transformation, much like a tree shedding its leaves, and it is the only way we can truly heal. Letting go is also allowing what we once thought was the road to our happiness to change direction.

The moment I decided that I was going to let go of what didn't serve me, I felt an instant weight off my shoulders. It's not that I didn't care anymore; in fact I cared more than I ever had about what made me happy. It's not a cavalier or careless attitude to let go of self-limiting beliefs. I feel empowered by the thought that I could connect with the source of my joy and happiness.

I realised I wasn't losing anything,

I was gaining.

Day by day I was gaining the ability to love myself, my true self. This is not physical; it cannot be bought or possessed, only experienced. Isn't that what everybody wants? I have to say that I would have absolutely laughed out loud if I had heard myself talking in this way before my cancer diagnosis!

To find peace in ourselves is our natural state, to be able to forgive ourselves and others from the heart, empowers our spiritual growth, and the ability to let it go, let it go, let it go...

Exercise

Letting Go

So, now you might be thinking, *'What can I let go of?'*
Luckily, I have a few ideas on this. Try this exercise to help let go (I learned this one from my yoga teacher too).

Find a comfortable space to sit (anywhere) and close your eyes.

Place your hands in your lap.

Breathe in and out.
Just simply notice your breath, don't try to change it, just notice it as it flows in and out. Watch it rise and fall.

Relax your shoulders, your face and jaw.

Open your ears to all the sounds around you, whatever they are.
A bird chirping, the noise of cars driving past, the sound of the washing machine and so on. Really tune in to this.

Stay in this space for five minutes, that's all you need to do.
You will notice a difference right away.

At the end of the five minutes think about what you are willing to let go of.... I think you may be surprised.

Ever tried?

Have you ever started something and never finished it? Ho hum, I am the queen of it (I still have a tapestry going that I started in 1987). Trying new things can be exciting and daunting the same time, but we actually start new things every day and don't think about it. We learn new skills (how to operate your coffee machine) we have new experiences (going to a shop we have never been in before) and we deal with things we have never done before (especially true when your teenage daughter asks for more pocket money).

Samuel Beckett's quote, *"Ever tried? Ever failed? No matter. Try again. Fail again. Fail better."* couldn't be more apt. Like anything when you are learning something new, it takes practice and patience. We bumble around to begin with, we're not sure but the more we do it the better we get at it. Think back to when you got your drivers licence, how crap were you at three point turns (I know I was) but as you practised day after day you got better.

I like the word 'snoopiness' because it conjures up the magical thinking that we had as children; to be curious is to engage with ourselves, ask questions and try new things (and I also love Snoopy the Dog!). If you are motivated to become curious about your life and the world we live in you will be willing to try different things, it's almost a by-product. Inspired thinking leads to an inspired life. I am so much more curious about many things these days, I'm always going out of my way to expand my horizons and I love this new-found approach to my life. I have become quite the nosy parker actually. I am fascinated by everything.

We all have this ability, to ask questions, to try our hand at something; it's not time consuming, or all-consuming on our mind; it's fun and makes us ask ourselves questions. Sometimes they are just little questions, sometimes big ones, but as we inch our way towards knowledge, we find ourselves miraculously knee deep in something that we had never been interested in before. This book is a testament to this exact concept. I had never been interested in any of the topics I cover (well, maybe a few) but until I started to become curious, I was unaware of just how much I could learn and the impact it would have on me.

≈ ≈ ≈

I too am also a creature of habit (ask Jo, I have the same breakfast every Sunday morning, two eggs over easy, on gluten free bread) and while there is comfort in that, I'm also very mindful of trying to reignite my mind and its habits by taking myself out of my comfort zone and trying new things. We can become rather lacklustre if we continually do the same thing over and over again and we ultimately get stuck in the rut of tedium. I am the queen of this too, monotony, I do like things to be in some type of order in my life. Chaos makes me a bit nervous actually, but I have learnt to live with it a lot more than I used to. I have learnt that it isn't necessary to be in control of everything in your life and that doing things differently is a reason to celebrate and move into a new comfort zone, one that has plush pillows and all-you-can eat platters of cheese please! It's a place I rather like now; I like to call it my new comfort station.

Living an inspired life means you also have to stick at it and get in touch with your own thoughts. I try not to think about it as an arduous task (sometimes my mind is a wide open space full of tumbleweeds) instead seeing it as a challenge: "I am learning something new and that's awesome". I also try not to beat myself up if I don't seem to be 'getting' it quickly, I know I won't be perfect on the very first day I begin something new, I am doing my very best and, in my book, that's a great start.

So, why is it when we say to ourselves "I am going to start living the life of my dreams", we fall in a heap and think we cannot do it. Somehow we don't even get past the start line?

When I decided that I would pursue my dream of becoming a full time writer, I thought I had gone a little bananas really. How was I going to do that? Yikes, it was just a dream, I couldn't possibly do it.

There is a saying "Nothing changes if nothing changes". I love this. It sums up life really. If you are afraid to change, then nothing will change. Don't get me wrong, I deliberated for nearly twelve months about whether I could make real changes in my life, I had to think very carefully about the how, when and if! We are all here to strive for something and no matter what it is, we undoubtedly at some point fall short of the expectations we set ourselves. And that is OK. This is how we learn and how we pick ourselves up off the floor when something doesn't go quite to plan. What actually stops us is the fear of failure.

We don't try because we think we will fail.

The word failure means 'lack of success', a strange concept really because if we didn't fail from time to time, we wouldn't learn and we wouldn't grow our inner awareness about how to make changes in our lives. This is how we learn.

Why are we so frightened of failure? We will fail, that's a given, everyone does. To recognise what we are doing wrong is part and parcel of becoming better at something and being successful in the end.

It is courageous to fail; in fact, the words we often hear should be "*Facing failure is brave, to accept it is brave and to use it is even braver*".

Time to share my story with you here.

This book is actually the fourth I have written, two of them have been published, one hasn't. I have been inspired by many topics and subjects over the years and each one of my books covers a certain time in my life and my observations and memories. The Leap Year was a deeply personal book about my breast cancer journey while Four for the Road delved into the world of travel writing about a road trip I took with my husband and teenage children around the UK and Scotland.

After the success of having these published I was on a roll, thinking to myself, wow, I'm not too bad at this writing business. Yippee! Maybe I got ahead of myself, maybe I was too cocky, I don't know, but my third book was knocked back by my publisher. I was gutted. That book was about my Christmas stories. I absolutely love Christmas, it's my favourite time of the year. Christmas is awesome and I never miss a magical minute of it (even if that means a few tears in the tinsel). I wanted to write about all of my favourite Christmases: it's a special time for everyone, a time for families and friends to gather, share joy and compassion, and take a break from everyday cares. I thought that my stories were entertaining, heartfelt and quite funny. So when no one else thought that, I realised that I still had a lot to learn.

So, it was back to the proverbial drawing board for me.

It did knock the wind out of my sails for a bit, I actually didn't write anything for months. I used to sit at my computer and try to write but nothing came, I wasn't inspired to write about anything and I couldn't concentrate. I thought, 'Is this it? I'm a two-book wonder; I'm going to have to find something else to do, maybe this isn't my path after all'.

I had already decided to leave my full time job and to say that I was freaking out would be an understatement. What if I had got this completely wrong, maybe people were just telling me that I was a good writer but secretly thinking 'She is totally in the wrong career'? What have I done?

By this time I was only weeks out from leaving on a holiday and I thought, 'Well let's wait until I get back from my trip and see if something pops up to inspire me'. And it did. I have been asked many times about life after cancer. I hadn't given it a whole lot of thought actually, I was just getting on with my life. It wasn't until someone said that they thought I was 'amazing' (I know, massive compliment!) that I realised that maybe there is something in this.

Could I write about what changed in me after having cancer? And maybe other people want to know how to move on after a life changing event?

As soon as I got back, I was on my computer and typing away like a mad woman, I couldn't get my words down quickly enough. So the moral to this story is, TRY AGAIN. The other moral is that you can do anything you put your mind to, and soon you will find that you will be on your way to starting something fabulous (and actually finishing it). Now, where's that tapestry?

≈ ≈ ≈

Changing your life is not a lot different. You have to try. What's the worst thing that could happen? I know, you could be living in a tent, but truthfully, if you make the decision, it will be the right one because you made it.

There is no time like the present.

You can make change and learn this very moment, commit to yourself that you will learn something (or a series of things) once a month—anything my friends—from learning a new program on your computer to learning a new language.

Give yourself permission to try, it doesn't matter where you start, and it certainly doesn't matter if you stumble.

Down dog

"My name is Jane Delahay and I'm a yoga tragic."

I don't think there is a weekly meeting to announce that you are a yoga addict but I certainly would fit into that category if there was.

Recently I found a little quip about yoga (you know those little 'make your day' memes) and it said, *"Reasons why I am currently alive: Yoga, Coffee and Wine"*. LOL, this **IS** why I'm currently alive. I love it, that really tickled my funny bone. I am a yoga tragic. I sought solace in the practice of yoga during the time of my diagnosis and it proved to be my saviour.

I cannot overstate what a difference yoga made to me in those first few months of chemotherapy. It was such a blessing (and a luxury) to give myself an hour of just 'me' time, to spend time with myself. I honestly thought that putting me first was a selfish thing to do but I know now through my yoga practice that you cannot be your best self if you don't spend any time with yourself. To be completely at ease with yourself is something that I had never experienced before.

The rectangular mat that I roll out on the floor every yoga class should be called the 'magic carpet mat', because whenever I get on it, I feel that a wonderful ride is about to happen. Yoga has become a big part of my life, I started with only one class a week during chemotherapy, I increased that to two classes a week during radiotherapy and then to three times a week during the last few months of immunotherapy. Fast forward three years and I now do six classes a week. I am totally addicted to yoga (not a bad thing to be addicted to!) I do a combination of Vinyasa, Slow Flow and Yin. By doing something as simple as a few pretzel poses (and a bit of huffing and puffing) I have got to know my body's abilities and potential—and limitations! I know so much more about myself and the way my body mind works. The relationship I now have with myself is miles away from the one I had three years ago. I have got to know the real me and I like her. Boom! What an awakening I had, it's quite marvellous and one of the best things is that sense of connection I also have with the world around me.

Tuning into the elements of the universe through my yoga practice has been an enlightening journey. I have learnt so many things about our natural world that up until then I pretty much ignored or saw as a negative not a positive, like the rain. Everyone always complains about the rain, but now, I look forward to the sound of rain, it's one of life's pleasures listening to the falling rain on your roof.

The Earth element is my favourite because it keeps our ego in check. It has a grounding and calming effect on our minds. It's associated with the Root Chakra which governs survival, security and our place in the world. I have identified a lot with this chakra; it represents the connection to the power of Earth Mother, providing us with the ability to be grounded and to feel safe.

When I was diagnosed with breast cancer I felt that my world had been ripped out from underneath me, my stability had gone and I was no longer feeling safe in my own life. The Root Charkra holds the basic physical needs for survival, the foundation of life—

and mine was crumbling before my eyes.

I know it sounds all a bit hokey, but yoga has taught me how to connect with the essence of myself through the awareness of these energy flows, the vital life force that we all have. I have spent quite some time now delving into the reasons I felt so unbalanced in my life: a lot of it had to do with blockages and dysfunction in my own energy flows. I knew there was something wrong a few months before my diagnosis, I felt strange in myself, spacey and foggy in the mind and very much out of balance. I felt like I was just going through the motions of life and I wasn't inhabiting or being present in my own life. Geeez…

Writing this now is a little sad for me because I know that I didn't trust myself at the time. I didn't trust that there was something wrong, I had all but forgotten about connecting with myself, I had forgotten what an engaging and meaningful life was, and I had such dissatisfaction with not only my own life but the world around me. I was not present in my own freaking life. No wonder I was feeling like crap.

As a massive convert to the practice of yoga, I still cannot believe how much this ancient practice has changed my life. That's why I say yoga was my saviour, it's not just about exercise, it's a practice of self-awareness, self-love and committing myself to something that gives me joy every day. Yoga is more than just our thinking minds. It's a whole experience, the way we connect, how we speak, how we incorporate and internalise ourselves, and the realisation that the true self is not always physical.

Yoga has had a bit of an explosion in recent years in our Western World, more people practice yoga now than ever before. Apart from the meditative and mindful aspect of yoga, it allows us to tap into our intuition, something we ignore for most (or all) of our lives. To be consciously in touch with our intuition is very powerful.

The role of intuition in our day-to-day lives is more important than ever. Intuition is about connection, the connection to our inner selves, our universal self and each other. But it's easy to become disconnected from our intuition with the fast paced lives we lead. Yoga brings me back to the place where I can connect and keep myself in balance and harmony. It's about listening to that intuition and using it to recognise that we are falling off the wagon into an unaware life and we need to correct our path to one of stillness and reflection.

To be in that place of quiet contemplation is indeed a calm place for me. I come up with great ideas in this space; I make peace with myself and have an appreciation of what really matters in my life. It makes me smile, and that's gotta be a good thing.

Exercise

Falling in love with Yoga

Before you go rushing off to the closest yoga studio, here are a few thoughts for you.

- Take a look around your neighbourhood for a studio (it's best to be either close to work or home).

- Try out the introductory/free specials (all studios have them).

- Do a few different styles of yoga to see which one suits you.

- It is really important to connect with your yoga instructor; if you don't, try another class.

- You don't need super expensive outfits (discount department stores do great yoga gear).

- Commit to classes you can attend (this may only be once a week, and that's awesome).

Yoga is about your own practice and it takes time. Be patient with your body, it's not a competition. Yoga has been around for thousands of years, it has by far been the best 'find' of my life and my happy place. I urge you to consider getting on board with it; I think you may just fall in love.

I also cannot overstate the value of a yoga retreat, I have been on two now, but it was certainly not something that had ever been on my radar. On a wing and a pranayama I signed up for a yoga retreat a few years back, not just around the corner mind you, in Greece on the island of Hydra. In my usual way, I ploughed head first into something I knew nothing about, didn't have the budget for and I had no idea how I was going to physically do five hours of yoga a day.

When it comes to retreats, depending on what you fancy, the sky's the limit. You can in all seriousness go to a yoga retreat in the French Alps (no après skiing mind you) or in Marrakech (this one offers cake, not sure why that would be a highlight unless you had been on a no sugar diet for a while). Pretty much the only reason I chose the yoga retreat I did was because I just adore my teacher. She had just returned from a retreat in Greece and absolutely raved about it. It just sounded so magical that I was swept up with the excitement of it all and signed on the dotted line as soon as I could. The website description, "Set against a backdrop of bougainvillea and exquisite Mediterranean views, Hydra is full of cobblestone streets, traditional tavernas, a crescent shaped harbour and is known for its beauty and old world charm", sounds perfect doesn't it?

I had heard only positive stories about retreats, generally about how wonderful people had felt afterwards: "Everyone should do a yoga retreat, they are better than holidays!" People talked of it changing their perspectives, understanding their truer selves, changing their habits and attitudes, the list goes on. I was listening with open ears. I had just signed up for one and I was getting more excited as the days passed. The one aspect I was most interested in was how focusing on their yoga practices had changed their lives. So, how could spending a week doing five hours of yoga and meditation a day help me even more? Well I was just about to find out.

For the first time I was combining two of my loves, travel and yoga. But for me the most exciting part of travel is the planning. When you book a trip you instantly have something to look forward to, it's like all your Christmases have come at once. You have chosen your destination and now comes the fun bit, filling in all those gaps with daydreams of gorgeous cobblestone streets, eating beautiful food at a local taverna, wisteria-laced pergolas shading you from the afternoon sun and swimming in the aqua blue water. You can see it in your mind's eye, just how you imagined it. The bubble of excitement is magical, it's like stargazing, you are mesmerised and little jolts of joy fill your being. The fact that it can go on for months (depending on how far in advance you book your holiday) is a feeling I never tire of.

Unfortunately four weeks out from the retreat I still hadn't booked a flight, organised travel insurance or booked any transfers or accommodation. Not through laziness but lack of funds. I scraped together enough frequent flyer points to pay for the flight but the rest I'm afraid had to wait. And that meant pretty much right up until the day I left. With less than €200 in my pocket for my fortnight's trip away I left for the airport on public transport. I knew things would be tight and I was desperately hoping that I wouldn't starve (I love Greek food) but this was the first time I had left our shores with so little money. This did concern me, I had to be super savvy on this trip and it was going to test my resourcefulness. Breakfast was included in the accommodation and I hoped that I didn't have to start thinking of ways to hide pastries and fruit in my yoga bag.

Thirty other people had signed up for the retreat and apart from my yoga teachers I knew only two other people, and they were a couple. I am not a novice in the travelling solo stakes and I'm pretty accustomed to talking to strangers, but there was a small part of me that worried about spending the entire time on my own. I am not that fond of my own company (well in small doses, I'm sure most people would attest to the same quantity of time). I had the best of both worlds, travelling solo meant that I could be on my own or be with a group if I wanted to, I had a choice. I am not averse to travelling in a group either but unless you are totally compatible, there will be times when you wish you were on your own. The other members might think you're being selfish or you are embarrassed by them, any number of reasons really. I didn't have to deal with that at all; I could flit between groups or being all on my lonesome (I was desperately hoping not to be the lonely traveller all of the time). They were certainly a mixed bunch: couples, sisters, mums and daughters, groups of friends (six members in one of them) and to my surprise, two other solo travellers.

Fantastic, I wasn't the only one, and that meant at least I wouldn't be sitting at the breakfast table alone. It isn't that easy to immerse yourself in a large group when you have no wing-woman. I really had no idea what to expect, for in any large group you are invariably going to like some people and not others, that's just human nature. We all had one thing in common—yoga—but apart from that, we were from different upbringings, races, religions, socioeconomic and geographic backgrounds, we were the quintessential mixed lolly bag. 'What fun', I thought (and I really mean that). For me, meeting people is fascinating. I love hearing people's stories. That's what captivates me about travelling. You never know who you're going to meet. The retreat gave me the chance to reconnect with myself, unwind and focus on the real me and realise what was important for my own personal development. So if you are thinking about attending a yoga retreat, I say go for it!

P.S Through some super savvy budgeting on my behalf, I came home with €2 in my pocket.

An attitude of Gratitude

I discovered the practice of gratitude during my cancer treatment. When my husband first suggested it, I thought it sounded all hokey and quite frankly, I didn't want a bar of it. It was challenging some days to feel like I had anything to be grateful for, I struggled with it, I honestly thought that I had nothing to be grateful for. How could I be grateful when all I could think about was the shitstorm I was living in.

Acquainting myself with the feelings of gratitude was not one that came automatically to me, I had to work at it. I found it easier to write it down than think it in my mind. I remember sitting there thinking, 'Really, is this what it's come to? I'm writing a list of things that I feel grateful about?' WTF!

I used to get embarrassed about what I'd written, I felt stupid feeling grateful for my dog for instance. Really? Is my dog feeling grateful back? Probably, because he is a dog and I feed him, walk him and pick up his poo. Who wouldn't be grateful for that? And my favourite, being grateful for being me. Really? I know I'm me. What exactly am I grateful for today? Oh, yes, I had nearly forgotten, I'm grateful that I have to have a needle stuck in my arm tomorrow.

I used to have these conversations with myself all the time when I was writing my gratitude list. (Actually I still have them.) As you can see, I didn't take to it as easily as I could have. My sense of sarcasm and irony was leading the way rather than an appreciation for realising that I could take responsibility for redesigning my own life.

Gratitude by definition means "the quality of being thankful". I began to notice that other people were also recommending the daily practice of gratitude in their blogs and online. I thought to myself, *'maybe there is something to this gratitude thing, is it really a magical way of life?'*

When you're faced with a life challenging situation you'll do almost anything to get your way through it. What's the worst outcome it could give me? (at least I had a few of those nice notebooks to write in, that's something to be grateful for.)

So I pursued it—and to be honest, it works. This is no weird hocus pocus thing after all. It took some practice and sometimes a little while to think about what I had to be grateful for (besides me and my dog). But over time I began to notice and be grateful for all the good things around me, no matter how big or small. Gratitude is a powerful emotion and it's a gift that keeps on giving.

When I used to find myself in that overwhelming state of turmoil during treatment, being grateful helped me see things a little more clearly. Bringing gratefulness into my daily life was an important part of my recovery. It gave me the chance to stop and take time to open myself up to what was good in my life.

Gratitude has become a way of life for me now and I consciously choose to live my life according to those principles. I have found it to be deeply rewarding to live my life this way. By showing gratitude for the things around me, I stopped being so consumed about what was happening to me. In a way it reversed my thoughts: by concentrating on what's good, the difficulties didn't feel quite so bad. Stepping away from those feelings of dread and turning them into a positive experience gave me space to open my heart to my own good fortune.

Feeding our brain with gratitude makes us feel better—it's just the way our brains work. If you practise gratitude you will become more grateful. By feeling this way I was letting off better chemicals in my brain than the ones that made me sad and fearful.

Each year I now do a top 20 gratitude list; this is my 2018 edition of what I'm grateful for (in no particular order):

1. My beautiful husband and children
2. Yoga, it's still my new love even after three years
3. My dog Raffy, even if I have to pick up his poo
4. My Birkenstocks, they are pillows for my feet
5. Trekking Tuscany with my big sister
6. Visiting the magical island of Hydra
7. Sunrises
8. My girlfriend Jo
9. Succulents (they are so much easier to grow)
10. The Marilyn's (my sisterhood)
11. Mastiha (a delicious Greek alcoholic drink)
12. Eyebrow pencils
13. My hair, for not going grey
14. My family and extended family
15. Photobooks
16. Reflexology, more pillows for my feet
17. My health
18. Gold Class cinema seats
19. Turning 50 (yippee, I'm proper grown up)
20. Toasted coconut

≈ ≈ ≈

On top of my grateful tree is the ability to travel this amazing planet of ours, travel really puts things into perspective for me. I realise just how trivial and tiny my problems are. I'm a sucker for a travel quote and one of my favourites is "Fill your life with adventures, not things. Have stories to tell, not things to show". My practice of gratitude has sure made me realise that when you focus on what is good in your life, the good gets better. I want to tell you a story from one of my recent trips.

I fell in love with Rosa the moment I saw her. Rosa is a cat. Yes, a cat that lives in Hydra. I happen to think we can learn a lot from our furry friends. I spent quite some time alone on my recent trip to the Greek island of Hydra and it gave me the chance to not only reflect but to observe the wonderful world happening around me.

Cats are part of the landscape in Hydra; they come in all shapes and sizes, colours, personalities and states of health. They are definitely free range on the island; the locals take care of them in their own way by putting food out for them and the restaurant owners leave scraps for them after their patrons leave for the night. But here's the thing. They live harmoniously among one other, they belong to no one and they roam freely without care or cause. What a wonderful way to be. I found myself endlessly fascinated by the cats of Hydra. I took so many photos of them I could publish a photo book (maybe I will!). I'm a cat lover from way back; I grew up with cats and have two of my own. They are such mystical creatures and perfect in every way.

Without sounding like a crazy cat lady, these are the lessons I learnt from Rosa (and all the other cats on Hydra):

- Find your place to stand (or lie), your place of inner peace.

- It doesn't matter what you look like (black, white, tortoiseshell, ginger) or what the person next to you is doing, be you.

- From that place decide what it is that makes you, you.

- Redesigning yourself is the definition of what it means to live your life your way and live free range if you want to.

- Everything is possible (even lobster for dinner).

- Stay connected to your spirit, catch the moment of what really makes you happy (and lie in the sun).

- Take care of yourself, nourish you.

- Be kind to others (and share your food!).

- Stop to wonder, take in what is around you and really look and be present.

Cats are known to be graceful, skilful, nosy and outgoing. I like to think that we can adopt their characteristics into our own lives with more wonder and wisdom. I think there is a lesson in that for all of us.

Exercise

The art of Gratitude

So how do you practise the daily art of this gratitude thing? It's actually very simple and takes no time at all.

Every day I write down three things that I am grateful for, what happened or I noticed during the day.

It matters not how small or large. I just jot down three things, any old thing really; keep it simple, that's it.
Why not give this daily practice of gratitude a try.

Do this every night (or morning) for a month and then at the end of the month reflect on how you are feeling.
Have you noticed any changes? I hope so. I know I did.

Use the following pages to kick off your gratitude for a month

Write down how you are currently feeling.

_____
_____
_____
_____
_____
_____
_____
_____

3 things I'm grateful for today

Day 1

1.

2.

3.

Day 2

1.

2.

3.

Day 3

1.
2.
3.

Day 4

1.
2.
3.

Day 5

1.
2.
3.

Day 6

1.
2.
3.

Day 7

1.
2.
3.

Day 8

1.
2.
3.

Day 9

1.
2.
3.

Day 10

1.
2.
3.

Day 11

1.
2.
3.

Day 12

1.
2.
3.

Day 13

1.
2.
3.

Day 14

1.
2.
3.

Day 15

1.
2.
3.

Day 16

1.
2.
3.

Day 17

1.
2.
3.

Day 18

1.

2.

3.

Day 19

1.

2.

3.

Day 20

1.

2.

3.

Day 21

1.

2.

3.

Day 22

1.

2.

3.

Day 23
1.
2.
3.

Day 24
1.
2.
3.

Day 25
1.
2.
3.

Day 26
1.
2.
3.

Day 27
1.
2.
3.

Day 28

1.

2.

3.

Day 29

1.

2.

3.

Day 30

1.

2.

3.

What changes have you noticed?

≈ ≈ ≈

The words *'thank you'* are underrated. We don't use these two words enough in our daily lives. How many times a day do you say thank you? It's something to think about because we probably don't say it enough.

I'm a lot more aware of this now and I am astounded when I see people in cafés say nothing to the person who is serving them. It's rude and shows a lack of compassion, thoughtfulness and kind-heartedness. I have to stop myself from standing up and saying, "Have you forgotten something?"

We all know how lovely it is to receive a compliment or special attention from someone. When we give thanks we are showing appreciation for something or someone. Saying thank you makes people feel happy, full stop. Remember when your mum said, "Don't forget the magic words"? She knew how important the words 'thank you' are for your life. They are indeed magical. To give thanks is to be grateful and gratitude is a powerful thing. Saying thank you gives you a real sense of well-being, it brings you closer to other people and closer to yourself. It's a very simple thing to do and it's free. There are no attachments to it; we do it because we want to (and we should).

Exercise

Say Thank You

Try saying a few of these things throughout the day to yourself and others (there's no limit):

Thank you for my coffee.

Thank you for your note.

Thank you for doing a great job.

Thank you for being awesome.

Thank you for the flowers.

Thank you for coming to my party.

Thank you for being you.

Make the words 'thank you' part of your everyday vocabulary. I suspect once you start using them more often you will make someone's day (and your own).

Shiny Happy People

One of the lines to the song *Shiny happy people* suggests that there's no time to cry. Hmm, life is certainly not happy and shiny all the time; there are tears, lots of them. (Cry me a river would be more apt).

I wrote this chapter last because it's hard to write about being happy. I had skipped past this chapter many times and thought 'I'll get to that one later' and as time went on, I thought 'Maybe I will delete this chapter, I have no idea what to write'. No one wants to hear about how it's easy to be happy: "No problem, just be happy", they say. Sure no problem, I will turn my frown upside down, there smiling!

Feeling happy has not been easy for me; I thought I could just turn a 'happiness' switch on and all would be dandy. "Nothing to see here, I've just turned on some good old fashioned happiness for myself." Yeah right.

That feeling eluded me for many years. I had pockets of happiness but true exhilaration for life was hardly my default position. I used to think that everyone around me was happy, and I was the only one who wasn't. Isn't happiness our natural state? What is happiness really? If you are not happy does that mean that there's something wrong with you? Is happiness just a fleeting thing that comes into our lives occasionally, like a flitting butterfly in the summer? I cannot even begin to answer those questions—I am certainly not an expert in this field—so I will tell you about what makes me happy and how I made room for the shizzle thoughts I was having.

Instead of trying to block them out, I used them to create a more meaningful life, yes meaningful, not happier (cause I don't think there is such a thing as being happy all the time).

For me happiness is contentment. I like this word a lot better. It was about just being comfortable about what was going on in my life, regardless. I created my own state of well-being by choosing my thoughts, my own realities, and choosing to be in the state of ease and not despair.

I'm not saying that was easy, I think you know from my story that happiness was not a word I bandied around a lot but I truly believe that life is not supposed to be mission impossible either, life is meant to be happy, and being in a state of satisfaction certainly made me feel better.

I've learnt that contentment is always available, it's not hiding anywhere but it was on long service leave when I got sick. I found it difficult to embrace myself and my life; I knew there was something wrong. Happiness should have been something I accepted and allowed to be part of my everyday life, not something I had to 'find'. "Hello, knock knock, any happiness going on in there?"

I know it isn't realistic to be happy all of the time; our lives consist of light and dark, seasons, reasons, progression, sadness, enjoyment and balance. No one's life is always on the rise and rise; we need to be OK with the roller coaster ride.

I believe that we are here on this earth plane to learn, be challenged, and if that means stumbling a few times, then I consider it a good thing. By choosing contentment we needn't silence our other emotions either. Our daily lives can be the full monty of emotions (I know, my dog vomits on the carpet too) but our thoughts dictate how we feel about it. Let those feelings move through you. Our thoughts are just thoughts—remember the cloud analogy? Let them pass.

I try not to have feelings of disappointment at these times, I make room for them and create a life despite them (I am human after all).

Exercise

Meaningfulness... or is that Happiness?

These are some of my tips for creating a more meaningful life and I do each and every one of these things on a regular basis.

~ Bond with people

This is your community, other human beings, we are meant to spend time together, and we're all in the same boat. It gives us the feeling of security and involvement. Make time to genuinely connect with people.

~ Help other people

By making time to be actively involving in a charity, community or club we are opening ourselves up to the benefits of belonging and having a sense of purpose. It's a wonderful feeling when you help others, and it's just a damn nice thing to do.

Giving is one of my real purposes these days, it gives me a lot of joy to give my time, money and love to people, animals and the planet. Even when my own chips are down, I still find ways to give back, whether it's my time, positivity or a donation. I truly believe that giving is the circle of joy: the more you give, the more comes back to you.

~ React positively

It's not necessarily what happens in your life but how we react to it that counts. As I said before, you are in charge of how other people make you feel. Train yourself to expect the best in every situation, be optimistic and hopeful in everything you do. Regardless.

When I was diagnosed with cancer, it was a shock (for sure) but I tried to think about the positives of my situation as much as possible (it wasn't easy) but I now know that this helped me get through what was the hardest road in my life. I chose to see the positives in a really shizzle situation. After all, we are what we think about: so think good thoughts.

~ Start something... anything
We are all guilty of getting stuck sometime in our lives. We simply need to take action, it doesn't matter what it is, just move forward. Start that course, create a to-do list, make that phone call, visit that place you have been dreaming about, get to work on something.

Starting anything is the first step, taking action will immediately make the situation better and you will feel more in control.

Peace and Quiet

When I was a child I used to ask my parents for suggestions of what gift they wanted for their birthdays, and their answer was always "Peace and quiet". Ha ha! I do understand this now I am a parent myself but now the best way for me to access peaceful tranquillity on a regular basis is with my reflexologist and acupuncturist. I know, I hear you saying, "Here she goes again, who even goes to a reflexologist?" I do, and I love it.

Integrative medicine is not new but it is gaining traction particularly in relation to managing cancer treatment side effects. Holistic health programmes are popping up in some of the world's best cancer hospitals, and I think that is awesome. I know first hand what it's like to manage the effects of weekly chemotherapy and let me tell you, it's not for the faint hearted.

I welcomed complimentary therapies when I was trying to minimise the impact of chemotherapy and radiation on my mind and body. Initially I started acupuncture to combat the fatigue and manage chemotherapy-induced menopause. I was determined to give myself the best chance at recovery and I am glad that I started researching this ancient (and drug free) therapy.

I attribute the fact that I lived a relatively 'normal' life during my treatment to acupuncture, yoga and reflexology.

Mind and body therapies now play an important part in my life because they improve my ability to interact and understand my 'whole' body, not only helping me cope with my cancer diagnosis but also to offset some of the nasty side effects that I was faced with. Coping with my diagnosis on an emotional level was paramount to my overall well-being; I really am not sure how I would have survived without the addition of these healing practices, they too saved my life. Learning and practising these mind–body techniques helped me overcome and build resilience, particularly after treatment ended.

I started to see my reflexologist a few months after I had finished cancer treatment. Menopause was still giving me grief (cue plenty of spontaneous sweating). I had read that when Louise Hay had been diagnosed with cancer she starting investigating healing herself and one of the treatments was reflexology. I didn't have cancer any longer by that stage but I wanted to give myself a cracking good chance that it wouldn't come back. I started to explore this alternative therapy and found a practitioner that lived nearby.

I had absolutely no idea what to expect, I didn't know anyone who had been to one, and so I thought, 'Hey why not? Let's give this a try? What's the worst that could happen? At least I'll get a foot massage', and, now I cannot think of my life without it.

Reflexology is a form of manual therapy using the fingers to work reflexes on the feet, hands and face. Each reflex corresponds to various organs, glands and structures in the body. By applying pressure to these points in the body reflexology helps to clear energy blocks, increases circulation and helps the body restore its natural balance which aids in healing. I like to think of it as pillows for my feet, it really is the most relaxing and rejuvenating thing to do.

I am not a massive 'foot' person, and by that I mean, I really don't like people touching my feet and the thought of touching anyone else's feet sends me into a spin. Feet are gross. Especially ones that have cracked heels, dirty soles, bunions, broken nails and blisters (erghhh). I look after my feet because the thought of looking down and seeing aforementioned foot conditions makes me feel woozy.

I admire my reflexologist and her ability to touch others people's feet; like podiatrists, it is not a job I would put my hand up for (or foot for that matter), but I'm glad she does because there's something quite lovely about having your feet massaged. It's kind of dreamy actually, it's like all those little pressure points activate a flurry of well-being. A sense of peace just envelops me, my whole body relaxes and I feel like I'm floating on a cloud (usually by that stage I am snoring too).

I talk a lot about taking 'time out' from day-to-day stresses, and reflexology is one of the best ways to just 'be'. There's nothing to do, nowhere to be, nothing to worry about except enjoying being in your own peaceful place.

My reflexologist works from home; she has this gorgeous little room at the back of her house that smells divine (mostly like lemon myrtle which I love) and it is decorated in pale green which I'm sure is from the 'serenity' palette and includes the most plush and luxurious blankets I have ever seen. She told me she got them from the supermarket! (I have looked for them but alas I have never found them). When I lie down on the table she wraps me in these blankets; it's like my very own comfort cocoon, I feel all warm and cosy and instantly feel Zen, even before she starts to work on my feet. She lets me choose my aromatherapy essence; my favourites are always citrus based because they are so uplifting. My reflexologist specialises in facial reflexology which is like having a facial but only better. She has this uncanny ability to know just where the points are on my face that needs attention. She also has an array of miniature tools that she rolls over my face, which does feel a little bizarre; I likened them to the utensils children use to make playdough designs. They look strange but apparently they're used to get the circulation going. I don't mind, it's all part of the relaxing nature of this heavenly treatment.

Visiting my acupuncturist is not a dissimilar experience except she doesn't have the posh blankets and she doesn't work from home. Her wellness centre focuses on well-being, both spiritual and emotional, and incorporates holistic solutions to everyday life. I like the phrase she uses "Ancient healing in a modern world". She is very chatty, exuberant and a little frantic at times, the opposite of my reflexologist who is calm and serene, but I like them both very much.

Acupuncture is part of Traditional Chinese Medicine and stimulates the nervous system to release hormones from the brain which improves blood and oxygen circulation. Acupuncture, just by the sheer fact that they are putting fine needles in your skin, isn't quite as relaxing. Depending on where the needles are inserted, you cannot move very much. This is particularly the case when the needle is sticking out from your ear. I have been known to doze off only to be awoken abruptly by a sharp sensation as my head is lolling around. But saying that, I usually do have a cat nap and feel amazing afterwards.

Both of these therapies are not instant fixes, you don't go there with a symptom, have treatment and then it's instantly better. It takes time for your body to feel the effects. I didn't walk away from my first treatment fist pumping the air and claiming that all my problems had gone. It was at least six months before I felt the benefits. I go regularly now to maintain my body's balance, and I know when I have left it too long, I start to feel anxious and 'out of whack' again, which is unsettling to me as this is how I felt before I was diagnosed. Acupuncture brings my equilibrium back and it's a place I welcome with open arms.

There's a lot of conjecture about whether reflexology and acupuncture actually work and whether it has been scientifically proven to be of any benefit. I'm not here to say whether it works for everyone or not, I can only tell you about my own experience, and that is that I have found it to be a very good addition to my well-being regime. I have for quite some time integrated western medicine with eastern medicine; it's the best of both worlds for me. I don't shun the advances that have been made in cancer treatment—I celebrate the fact that I am alive because of it—but I balance my western medicine with yoga, reflexology and acupuncture because it has helped me enormously in balancing my emotions, assists me in managing stressful situations and helps me manage living with menopause (as shizzle as it is).

Visiting my reflexologist and acupuncturist is also like seeing my very own counsellor. The first ten minutes of my visit is always about me. I get to talk about what has been happening in my life and then they offer up insightful advice or just listen. Both my practitioners are women and understand the challenges that I face, which I appreciate a lot. They both get it, they are working mums, they've had their own health scares and issues, and their empathy is very welcoming during times of anxiety. I love the fact that I can go there, sit on the couch and just chat, like we are having a cup of tea in a café. It is all very civilised and I don't ever feel that they are there to just do a job; they care about what they do and are passionate about helping people like me.

Maybe that's the attraction too, that it's a safe place to talk about how I feel and that I will never be judged for sounding like a crazy banshee. This is comforting and adds to my sense of well-being, and quite frankly sometimes I need all the help I can get. It's important to feel a connection with the person that you are spilling all your secrets and skeletons to; sometimes having a neutral person you can visit can take the worry out of seeking this sort of treatment. It's not mainstream and until recently was considered to be a bit bogus but my experience is that we need mind–body therapies to enjoy a higher quality of life and to embrace our own healing. I am a fan.

This way Up

What a drag stress is, I stick my fingers up at it. Stress is a killer—literally. It kills dreams, happiness, relationships and, in the end you, yikes! Stress is something that we all experience in our day-to-day lives. A little bit of stress is not a bad thing but a lot of it means you could be knock, knock, knocking on heaven's door. You do not want that.

Stress is defined as "pressure or tension", a word that is bandied around these days in relation to the crazy, stressed out world we live in. Our Western workplaces, homes, environments and lives are heading towards burnout, not chill'n out, my friends. So how do we combat this? We can't always just up sticks and move to the country and grow avocados. We know that we need to de-stress ourselves, but how can we do it in this ever increasingly obsessed world of ours that deems a successful life as one where we work eighty hours a week and is forever busy to one that embraces our well-being?

When we are stressed we struggle to see clearly or even think that there are any solutions to the problems facing us. Our thinking brain gets overtaken by the body's 'fight or flight' responses. As stress kicks in we find ourselves on the merry go round of fear, anxiety and panic, which ultimately starts feeding off one another. It's not a nice feeling. When it happens to me, my heart races, I start sweating and I feel dizzy. I was in a constant state of stress after I was diagnosed, my body buzzed, and not in the 'I have had five coffees today' way.

It was exhausting to feel so shaky and out of control but I didn't know how to stop it. In Ruby Wax's book 'Sane New World' she calls this the amygdala part of the brain (the emotional part) screaming at us. This part of our brain takes over, triggering a surge of cortisol and adrenaline. Yikes no wonder I felt fuzzy.

It is almost impossible to live stress free, actually it's impossible. We encounter stress on a daily basis—it's not going away anytime soon—so we have to accept it and start adopting practices into our lives to combat it. If you're anything like me, I still have a job, children to look after, a house to run and bills to pay; you cannot just stop living because you may encounter stress. What's probably more achievable is to lower the level of stress in our lives and be aware of how to manage it better. Recent studies have shown that stress can cause mental and physical fatigue, reduce concentration, reduce your body's immune system, distract your thinking and increase the likelihood of you getting sick. Pfft... that's not good news, so how can we manage stress in our daily lives to protect us against visiting frazzle town every day?

One of the best ways (I have found) to move towards a less stressed out life is through mindfulness and mediation (no eye rolling please!).

I touched on mindfulness earlier, but feel it relates to this chapter too. You cannot have too much of it in your life. Studies have shown that mindfulness is not only good for your soul, it calms and tames your mind so that you can see things with more clarity and understanding.

When activated early (when you notice you are stressed) mindfulness can deactivate the stress cycle.

Mindfulness takes time, quite a bit of it actually. I struggled to begin with and I am by no means an expert, but I feel my own experiences will help you see that it has enormous benefits for anything that our lives throw at us.

I was a bit of a sceptic at the start and I really didn't know what to do. When I first started my practice of mindfulness, I was halfway through fifteen months of cancer treatment; you can only imagine what my mind was like. Wild horses couldn't carry me away from the chaos in my mind. My mind was an untamed, uncontrolled, raging place that kept me up at night and trapped me in my own silent nightmare during the day. It was more of a necessity than a fleeting interest that got me started. I was barely functioning at that point and I needed to try something (anything). I was dangerously close to having a mental breakdown… and I needed help.

≈ ≈ ≈

It was by coincidence (or maybe not?) that my yoga studio advertised a course that very week on meditation and mindfulness. The course was two hours a week for four weeks. Bingo, time to reclaim my mind and my life.

I learnt a lot on that course, and it helped me regain some control of my thoughts and how to think more clearly. It wasn't about sitting still for hours on end until my legs went numb; it was about spending time being aware of what actually was going on in my head.

Anyone can meditate, really I mean anyone, even if you think that you couldn't possibly sit still for even a second or that you will be bored. You may be bored first up but you will start to have gaps in between which is where the magic really starts. You don't have to be like a statue sitting bolt upright either; I regularly scratch my nose, shift in my seat and cough whilst meditating, everyone does. It's not about being the best at it, my 'best' is pretty average really, I get distracted too, but in between are long peaceful breaks where I am really tuning into my mental state.

It has helped me sleep better, stress less and get stuff done. Mediating regularly has enormous benefits including heightening immunity and improving cognitive function. And all this takes less than 20 minutes a day. I hear you, "20 minutes? I don't have 20 minutes a day, I'm too busy". Consider the old Zen saying that we should sit in mediation for 20 minutes a day, unless we're too busy and that's when we should sit for an hour.

I have taken this knowledge and applied it to many things in my life now. I don't just practise mindfulness at yoga or during mediation, I mindfully walk my dog, I mindfully cook, I mindfully drive, I mindfully shop—get the picture? I am present in so many things in my life that my awareness is now tenfold more than it used to be; it has become almost second nature to me now.

I use the time first thing in the morning to meditate, that time before you get out of bed. I mindfully go through what I need to get done for the day and shuffle things around in my mind as I see fit. This is a much better way to start the day then leaping (or rolling) out of bed startled because you're late or worrying about whether you washed your favourite jeans.

≈ ≈ ≈

While we are on this topic of pausing, disconnecting from our devices is a must. I know, we didn't have to worry about it in the eighties but we do now. Our dependence on our smartphones is making it difficult for us to connect with not only ourselves but the people around us. The age of digital media is well and truly upon us. It surely does have some benefits (I love that I can stay in touch with my family that live OS).

The irony is that we now communicate with comments and emojis rather than face-to-face contact. We use social media to not only document our own lives but to peer into other people's. We see small snippets of other's lives, snapshots of what they want us to see. But we're only getting some of the story, we no longer have the connectedness that allows us to be fully present. We think we know a person from their Facebook posts but I would hazard a guess that they too apply a heavy hand to what photos they want the world to see (guilty as charged, I post photos that make me look good too!).

My girlfriend Jo calls this being a 'scroll zombie' which I think is quite apt. It describes the mindlessness that happens when we just stare at our smartphones and just scroll (and scroll...) and hit the like button. It really is a trivial and insignificant use of time, like we are on automatic pilot (which is another one of Mother Nature's gifts that we are mostly unaware of and probably should be). We are all guilty of it (me included) but becoming aware of the time spent on digital devices is paramount to creating the balance we so desperately want in our lives. I read recently that teenagers spend up to eleven hours a day with some sort of electronic device, yikes! I have teenagers myself and this is a scary statistic. Studies have also shown an increase in short term memory problems, eye sight issues, depression and sleep deprivation. If this doesn't make you want to start thinking about the time you spend on your smartphone then I don't know what does!

So, I say switch it off each night before you go to bed and make time during the day to have some digital downtime. Lower your stress levels today—your life depends on it my friends.

Exercise

Learning mindfulness

Just in case you were wondering about how mindfulness and meditation can be included in your life, I have put a few things together below,

Breath

Start with your breath, yes, that thing you do thousands of times a day. Breathing deeply slows the heart rate, relaxes the muscles and focuses the mind. Breath brings us into the present moment and a centred place. By concentrating on our breath, there's time to reflect on our priorities, problems and focus on what is important. Here are my favourite stress relievers: they are super easy to do.

- *Find a comfortable and quiet place to sit.*
- Put your hands in your lap and breathe in and out.
- Don't try to control it, let it happen naturally.
- After a few minutes, start to inhale through your nose and hold your breath.
- Then open your mouth and let it all rush out (you can even make a swooshing sound). Let the exhale become your release, let all of that stress out through your mouth.
- Do this ten times. You will feel uplifted at once. Try it.

Get Outside

...yes, that big wide world that we don't see when we work ten hours a day in an office.

- Make it a daily habit to get outside at least once.
- Lunch breaks are a good time.
- I'm sure that your neighbourhood has a park, walking track, garden, bench seat somewhere.
- Twenty minutes is all you need.
-

- Getting out into the sunshine has magical properties; we need it, not only for Vitamin D but to improve our mood.
- If you get the chance to go somewhere with grass, take your shoes off and walk barefoot in the grass, it is one of life's pleasures.

Stop

Yes, stop (I like to call it the pause button). Whenever you feel stressed, just pause, don't do anything for ten seconds. Create space, pause, think of it like a moment in time that gives you awareness of your surroundings and gives you access to choose a different course (very handy if you are about to say something you might regret).

Laugh

This is the easiest one. Download your favourite comedies and have a good ol' belly laugh.

Just Write

I have always been a bit of a jot it down kinda gal, to be fair. I've been writing to myself for years and it is a practice that has gotten me through some pretty crappy times in my life.

I keep three notebooks, each for a different purpose:
- My thoughts and brain dumps
- Interesting and fun facts
- Aspirations, daydreams and ideas.

It's my way of taking out what is in my mind and putting in on paper, it's cathartic and I encourage everyone to keep a journal (not 'Dear Diary' as such) but a place to write about your own stuff. Plus, I am getting worse at remembering things, so writing it down is paramount. If I see a great quote (for a book or article) I have to write it down there and then.

Once the domain of angst-ridden teenagers, keeping a diary or journal has now become the territory of many self-improvement experts—and for good reason. It's been scientifically proven that journalling can boost self-confidence and improve your immune system. Wow, who knew!

Journalling is all about your ideas that come up during the day, important things for you to write about and thoughts about your inner world. Think of it like your very own therapist, but a lot cheaper. I am personally addicted to writing; you don't have to be a professional to write; we can all do it.

Throughout the years I had been a bit on and off with journalling but I found myself madly scribbling down my thoughts when I was going through cancer treatment. I didn't do it because I had been told to (or that I read about it), it was something that was largely inherent and I felt safe to write down how I was feeling. I look back on some of my notebooks now and wonder what on earth I was writing about! I'm not even sure what *"licence to not care"* actually means! It doesn't matter; the fact that I had taken it out of my head onto to paper was enough.

Some days I would write the same things over and over, but it made me realise that I was ruminating over the same things day in, day out and that I was being rather pathetic and possibly a drama queen. Reading back on my own words was unsettling and confusing at first, I didn't know why I felt the way I did, and I was miles away from declaring that I was moving on from my cancer diagnosis. I was in an emotional no man's land, but the act of getting up each day and scrawling a few words across the page of my note book was therapeutic and an outlet for my grief, sadness and anxiety.

Who knows if this was my turning point, but I like to think that it had a part to play.

Writing has become somewhat of a dying art, well, handwriting anyway. Long gone are the days when we would sit and compose letters to our friends and family. In our hyper-connected word, with its Twittering and Facebooking, handwritten letters are practically extinct and I think that is an enormous shame. A handwritten letter is so personal; it's as close as being there in person. I have kept many letters, especially the ones from my grandparents; they're chock full of everyday things that seem mundane and minute, but they are fascinating to read now.

My grandparents are long gone but I have these beautiful messages and memories from them that only a handwritten letter can do. It's a physical reminder of them and I know that they put pen to paper all those years ago and wrote especially to me. That's what makes a handwritten message so powerful; it's the thought behind it, the fact that you are special. I used to love getting letters and postcards from my grandparents. Here's one from my grandmother from 1998:

> *"Dear Jane*
> *Just sitting here thinking of how everyone will be spread out all over the place instead of being here. I suppose you've heard about the stinking hot weather we've had, well today it's down to 20 degrees and it's cold but we've had nearly 24 hours of lovely rain, my poor roses just burnt to a crisp (honestly). I'll have to go out and cut them all off. I've been to the pool today, it was lovely and warm. I am back from New Zealand, it was a lovely holiday if a bit tiring towards the end. Trouble is I forget that I'm 76 and long days travelling are a bit too much but I wouldn't have missed it for anything. I saw 5 dolphins come out of the water not 2 yards away from me, I'll never forget that. Well, I'll take a walk and catch the post.*
> *   Love you, Grandma xx".*

Just reading these letters now, I have tears rolling down my cheeks. It's so wonderful that I have these memories of my grandmother. As I hold it I see her curly handwriting, her special writing paper with Australian flowers printed down the margin and I feel that she is still here, connecting with me through the written word. That is why it is so special to write. That is why it is so powerful. You cannot get the same range of emotions or the feeling of tangibility from reading a text or a Facebook post.

Receiving a letter makes us pay more attention to what is actually written than if we were to receive the same message by text. Because we have become so familiar with the distribution of messages via text, we no longer see them as anything overly interesting; in fact we glaze over the message and process less of what is in the message. I think we can all remember a time when we have received a text when our focus has been elsewhere; it dilutes the meaning and significance of what the person has sent to you. It could be important or a request, but we are too busy multitasking and checking out our Instagram at the same time. Paper-written letters force us to stand still, open it and actually read what's inside; it requires our attention, all of it.

In fact, writing is a kind of mindfulness. You have to be in the present moment, thinking about the person you are writing to. It takes concentration and commitment to sit still for a period of time and forge out a personal letter. Our attention is inward and we have to think about what we are going to convey. It isn't just a matter of sending a few emojis and some random "Hi, how are you?" We want to write something more meaningful and let our reader know that we are thinking of them.

But I get it, handwriting takes ten times as long, it's slow for the person to receive, but mostly it's because people are too busy. I think that embracing this old fashioned custom would really help us connect again with people and ourselves.

The idea that we can write about our lives and pass it on to our children as our own legacy is wonderful. I not only love the fact that I am reading my grandmother's words today, but that future generations will be able to read mine. Yikes, my great-grandchildren will be wondering who this crazy relative was!

Exercise

Writing it down

So how do you start journalling?
Start by just writing what's in your head. This can be anything, just scribble it down, it doesn't have to be the best handwriting or even words that make a lot of sense. It's the act of writing that clears your head and puts things into perspective. When you start journalling you may feel a bit weird. What's this, all this writing down how I feel? What do I even write about? You think, 'My pen is poised but I feel silly just writing anything'.

Here are some ideas to get you started:
- How was your day?
- Did you see someone you haven't seen for a while? How did that make you feel?
- Did you feel frustrated about anything?
- What did you see today?
- Was the sun shining, or was it raining?
- Did you contact that person you were going to?
- What colour will I paint my bedroom?

As you can see, you can write about anything! Even the weather can get a mention. Often, journalling starts and then falters because we expect too much. It doesn't matter that every page is not perfect and that our style and prose is not accomplished or even sensible. Whether you write about paying your bills, trauma or a love interest, they are your words—and that's what counts.

The best thing is that there are some gorgeous notebooks, pens and diaries out there. Treat yourself.

The simple act of writing a few words on a piece of paper can have an instant effect on your life and your well-being. Just write, your life will become more interesting.

A popular form of the written word these days are affirmations, I happen to like them (there I said it!). Affirmations are declarations of truth, your truth, no one else's. By repeating an honest and heartfelt affirmation, you encourage your subconscious mind to develop positive thoughts and feelings.

Affirmations are pretty cool. You can read them, write them, hear them or even play them to music; what goes on in our mind creates our life. The more you surround yourself with positive thoughts, actions and self-love, you will become more aware of the world around you and the things in it, including people.

There's no better way of repelling people you don't want in your life than with the buzz and passion for life that comes from repeating daily affirmations. You will shine my friends, and those that are blinded by your light will gently move away, to a galaxy far, far away...

Affirmations sound simple and they are.

When we first try to bring affirmations into our lives we may feel a bit silly. I know I did, it's like talking to yourself and hoping no one thinks that you have an imaginary friend.

Affirmations are words we say to ourselves, so be careful what you say! Much like mindfulness, they raise our awareness and verbally confirm our thoughts, aspirations and dreams.

Exercise

Affirming your Truths

Think of a garden, we plant tiny seeds and magnificent blooms appear (like magic). Our minds are the same, we have to plant tiny seeds to help nurture it. Send positive words to yourself and watch the beauty grow.

Grab yourself a pen and paper and write down six things that you want to feel immensely true about yourself.
They can go something like this:
- I am healthy.
- I believe in myself.
- I am beautiful.
- I deserve to live the life of my dreams.
- I am relaxed.
- I am super organised. (LOL, that's me!)

See how they all start with "I"? That's on purpose—you have to practise saying "I", like you are already that person. You see yourself as exactly what you are saying; it gives your affirmation strength, truth and reality.

Repeat your affirmations daily (even just once); say them, write them down, sing them, stick them on your fridge or use them as your screen saver.

If you are feeling a particular emotion, thought or feeling, then use affirmations to cheer you on. For example:
Doubt – I love my life.
Worry – I know how to relax.
Fear – I am protected.

Why not fill your mind with positive affirmations every day? They are really easy, they don't take any time and they instantly make you feel better. Go crazy with them, it doesn't matter what you write. Write anything but make sure they start with "I" and they will become your very own 'power belief system'... Wow I love that!

Of course, another form of writing that is very dear to my heart is writing books, just like this one. I am constantly thinking about things to write; sometimes they come to me in my dreams, and sometimes I wake up with a million ideas—and then promptly forget them once I've had breakfast. The one thing I know for sure is that I love writing and it doesn't matter what form that may take. Putting my thoughts down on paper (or on a computer) is a gift that's been bestowed on me and I take every opportunity to use it. I do think about this from time to time–did I always have this ability? Probably, I did after all do a double major in English in senior school and studied journalism and professional writing at university. I know!

Pursuing a creative career can be confusing because it doesn't fit nicely into the notion of being a real job. To be creative conjures up the notion that you must be either a little peculiar, love working with jute (or clay or some other medium) or you are no good at anything else. I still find it hard to say that I am a writer, which is actually now my job. I write stuff. Sometimes I feel embarrassed to say it because I fear that people will think that I'm flaky or that 'she doesn't have a real job'. I feel I have to justify myself and the career I've chosen. Whilst I make a small amount of money from selling books I am not in the league of the JK Rowlings of the world (but it is something to aspire to, for sure).

In the meantime I have to juggle all my other responsibilities on a financial level from a wage that is significantly smaller than my corporate income that I left behind. Creative careers are seen to be something you do before you get a proper job, not the actual job. Like a stop gap, or the oft-heard "She just needs to get that out of her system. Give her twelve months and she will be back in the corporate rat race like the rest of us" type of banter.

My girlfriend Jo tells me constantly that I am working hard in the present to secure my future and that is what I like to focus on.

(Thank goodness for her because sometimes I feel like she is my only supporter.) Writing a book is not an instant thing, I have in fact been writing this book for nearly ten months now and I devote most of my week to writing it, researching it, re-reading it or deleting it.

I would love to tell you that I sit here with constant inspiration and find it easy to do, but that wouldn't be the reality and I would be lying.

I daydream often and find myself staring out the window and wondering what on earth I'm going to cook for dinner. Life doesn't go away when you're writing, especially from home. My dog barks at every living thing passing by my front window, my children regularly text me (sometimes from upstairs, mind you) to ask for something (usually toilet paper), and my cat often thinks that my keyboard is a great place to have a snooze. I came back to my computer one day with the 'z' key stuck and a screen full of zigzags.

I am currently writing this in my dog-walking clothes, I haven't had a shower, the washing machine is going and I have just broken the arm on my glasses. Who said writing a book was glamorous?

I had little expectation about what my creative career would entail, but to be honest I did have a vision of me typing away here with a fancy computer and beautiful stationery. But the reality is more Second Hand Rose (as sung by John Farnham, Barbara Streisand and many others).

I have more bits of scrap paper and handwritten notes scattered across the table than a mad professor. Some days I'm looking under piles of paper just to find a quote or an article I read. It has to be here somewhere! I should probably have some kind of filing system for all these scrappy notes but I suspect that I would forget what section I put them under! I fortunately have my bookcase right behind me, making it extra handy when trying to find references, but for most part I am up and down from my chair, running a household, making cups of tea (that inevitably go cold) and trying to remember what on earth I was writing about before my cat coughed up a fur ball.

Don't get me wrong, I love it! I cannot think of anything that I would rather be doing than whiling away the hours writing stories and researching fascinating people and places. I feel so blessed and privileged to be doing what I love. This book is all about that. The fact I get to do this is awesome and I never take it for granted. Do you remember the time when you dreamed about where you are today?" I do.

Where did I park my Broomstick?

Some of the most intriguing things I have learnt about recently are (in no particular order) crystals, tarot, spirit, magic, moon cycles and spell work. Before you go "Geez, whoa, it's only chapter thirteen and she's totally lost the plot, what is she raving on about?" It might sound all a bit new age, a bit woo woo but I love it. I have for about eighteen months belonged to a Facebook group that is run by a witch. Yes, a witch, and I happen to think she is awesome. I'm not talking about stirring a cauldron and making potions here (although, how fun would that be!) she does sometimes wear a witches hat though! Her messages are insightful, uplifting, witty and she teaches us how to believe in not only the power of the universe and its magical abilities but also how our world can teach us more about ourselves and guide us to a life of meaningful purpose and understanding.

To be fair, I have always loved the 'witch world'. It's endlessly fascinating to me that we all belong to a world of possible magic. It's the stuff of fairy tales. I believed in them when I was child, and I believe in them now. There is a certain sense of comfort for me to know that there is something out there bigger than myself and that I can tap into it whenever I like, ask questions and receive answers. This ability has given me strength and reassurance in my life during times of real need. I know, you are probably thinking, 'Whoa! Has she has gone slightly bananas?' Well, I think that we all believe in something, I just happen to believe in magic.

To me, magic is about things that have no explanation, well not scientific ones anyway. Magic is a mysterious mistress. I am endlessly captivated about the notion that there is energy swirling around us in the form of angels, spirits and fairies. There's no other way to explain some of the things that happen to me on a daily basis. I constantly see things that confirm that am living in a magical world. I communicate with the universe regularly, sometimes it's just to say hello and sometimes it's "Please help me, I don't know what to do, please send me a sign", or something like that. The universe will pay me a visit in the form of a feather, numbers or sometimes try frantically to wave me down somehow so I don't miss the message. All of a sudden I see things I have never seen before, the universe doesn't want me to miss the opportunity and their message is sometimes loud and clear (I believe my cancer diagnosis was a sign).

I am always on the lookout for signs that are pointing me in the right direction. I have asked many times for help in writing this book for instance and I am rewarded with waking up in the middle of the night with just the right chapter already formed in my mind. When I receive communication like this I know that I am on the right track—the universe wouldn't trust me with this book if it didn't think I was capable. And of course, I don't always have a flurry of ideas, some days I sit here feeling very uninspired, fidgety and still in my pyjamas at midday. I may sit for an hour before I realise that I have written nothing and checked the weather channel twenty times. This, by the way is amusing, as my table faces a big window where it is quite obvious what the weather is doing. Other times I'm literally on fire, my typing simply can't keep up with the ideas cascading out of my brain. How does this even happen?

I do believe that if we are supposed to be doing something then it's easy, and vice versa if it isn't. The universe will block your path, or make things difficult if it isn't your calling. I know it sounds all a bit 'hufflepuff' but I honestly have no other way of explaining it. Let me give you a few examples.

When I wrote my first book '*The Leap Year*', I was not only super proud of it, I was confident that I would have the opportunity to collaborate with a notable not-for-profit organisation. I was absolutely sure that they would be on board, I initially asked them (politely) to promote my book on their website. I thought 'Fantastic, a targeted market for my book, what a great start'. They were interested to begin with but as time went on their enthusiasm waned. I would contact them whenever I thought there was any chance of working together; I was insistent and bordering on stalking by this stage. I sent email after email and never got a response. I used to count the days down until I could send another message, all the while hoping that I wasn't coming across like a desperado. I would find myself getting tetchy when I saw them collaborating with other people, not just well known identities but normal people like me. Why didn't they choose me? I must really suck and they probably hate my book and don't want to be associated with me.

Well, that's about the gist of what was going through my mind. Now I think back on that time, it wasn't meant to be. No matter how much I tried, the universe was blocking me. I had to let it go, this was not my gig.

And, this next story which made me quite upset at the time but

I know now that the universe had other things in store for me. You see, I was fired from a job that I didn't even get paid for, yes; I was sacked from a job as a volunteer.

I laugh about it now, but really? Who gets laid off from a job you do for free? I did. I couldn't even give my time away; nobody even wanted me to donate that. Talk about feeling crap. This was also not my gig, I thought it was, I absolutely loved my volunteering job but clearly I wasn't the person they were looking for.

Not that long ago I also realised something else that only the universe can explain. Every important event in my life is surrounded by the number 11. Every age that is a numerology calculation of 11 is when I have had major life changing events happen to me. Let me explain.

When I was 29, my husband and I moved to the UK to live permanently, leaving behind my family and friends. When I was 38 I was diagnosed with a rare type of congenital cyst which involved major thoracic surgery that took months to recover from, and when I was 47, I was diagnosed with breast cancer. The digits in each of these ages add up to 11, and they are the only ages that do so far in my life. I was also born on the 11th and I was married on the 11th. Isn't that just a little bit freaky? Or should I say enlightening? Actually I think it is magic.

I am totally intrigued by this; the number 11 is an angel number, especially 11:11 which is seen as a sign of synchronicity with the universe. Numbers are a universal language and they are around us all the time; have you ever glanced at your clock and it's 11:11? So what does this tell me? Well, that I was supposed to have these life changing events and they are my challenges to overcome, understand and take action from. I truly believe they happened for a reason. Stay tuned for when I turn 56! I feel this challenge will be a positive one.

I also think the universe has a sense of humour (in addition to firing me from my volunteer job). I cannot begin to explain why I hear David Lee Roth's *'Living in Paradise'* regularly on the radio; it's not exactly a top ten song, not now anyway. And David Lee Roth? What the? Well actually, he was a great lead singer in Van Halen and from memory he could do a high kick like no other, and he had great 80s' hair. I giggle to myself when I get in the car and hear that song again, and again, and again. To be fair, it's a banger of a song but I have started to really think about the words and the timing of when I hear the song; is the universe sending me a sign?

I have heard this song when I have had diabolically bad days and equally on awesome uplifting days. One example: I had to do the walk of shame at the supermarket and put my groceries back because I couldn't pay for them, I know, it was awful. The panic when every payment card I had was being declined made me turn a darker shade of embarrassment. I was mortified and couldn't get out of there quick enough. I got into the car and sat there nearly in tears. When I turned the key and radio started up, guess what was playing? At that very moment I could not have been further from living in paradise, but do you know what, it made me smile from the irony of it all. In fact by the time I turned out into the street I was laughing so much I had tears in my eyes.

To me, this song is about adventure, growing up and being free. Is that me now? Am I living in paradise? *Yes, I think so.*

≈ ≈ ≈

Intuition is something that I have connected with a lot over these past three years. Intuition is like an in-built super power, tapping into a different radio frequency if you like. I have become quite interested in spirit and sixth sense; it makes sense to me and it has helped me appreciate my life and understand the challenges that I have faced. Spirit is our consciousness and I have learnt how to live in this world with a renewed sense of purpose and how consciousness influences the way I live my life.

I talk about it a lot, how having cancer changed my life. I have spent hundreds of hours reading many different people's opinions, articles, books and texts as to why (and how) we face the challenges we do in our lives. The one that makes the most sense to me is that I was supposed to go through this: it is why I am here on this earth plane. I am here to learn and to teach others – a life purpose, if you like.

Yogis call it your dharma (your universal truth), and this was a very important part of my recovery from cancer. I have written about this before in my book *The Leap Year*.

Before I was diagnosed, I had no purpose, well, not one that was truly about me and my reasons for being on planet Earth. When I (finally) realised that I was here to become more spiritually evolved, it made sense. I wrote a few years back that I wanted to be a higher spiritual being and I wanted to help people. That IS my life purpose and, without sounding all evangelistic, it is what really changed my life—and yoga!

A few months back I attended a workshop about spiritual journeys. I had absolutely no idea what to expect. My girlfriend Jo and I went along with an open mind and if we could learn something, great, if not, we'd had a nice brunch in the neighbouring seaside town where it was held. I think I left there with more questions than answers, as some of the topics were really fascinating and some were downright old time woo woo. It was a small group, but all were there for different reasons. One person had lost a loved one recently and was searching for answers, others had had 'messages' from loved ones and didn't know how to interpret them, but for Jo and me, it was plain old curiosity.

One of the main messages I took away was that we are all here to learn, we are here to become spiritually evolved until we have learnt everything we need to learn. This can take ninety years or maybe even just a few years. And everyone's journey is different (this is the description of my journey I like, not the breast cancer journey…). I also learnt that even though you ask for your cup of tea with no sugar, that option is not on the menu.

Apparently, while our paths are not set in stone, our challenges are 'fixed'. We have the ability to make choices and steer ourselves to a different outcome, we are not always on automatic pilot. In my case, breast cancer was one of my challenges, but how I dealt with it was my choice, my free will. I feel very comforted by that thought; I had no choice that it happened to me. This was something that messed up my head for a long time, that I somehow was physically weak or I was unlucky, or worse, that I deserved it. Understanding that this was one of my life challenges helped me (and steered me) to the path that was meant for me. I needed to spiritually evolve and this was the universe's way of saying, "For goodness sake, stand up and listen Jane. You are on the wrong path".

Since then I have been very focused on my spiritual well-being through yoga and adapting my life to my true path. The fact that I am sitting here writing this now is testament to the knowledge I have gained through tapping into this inner world of mine. Communicating with and recognising the universe's messages is something I now do daily.

I listen to my intuition and when I cannot see or feel something, I ask for help.

If obstacles keep presenting themselves, I know that I'm not supposed to be doing it.

In the past I would pursue something that I 'knew' instinctively was wrong for me but I didn't know how to listen to or see the signs. I have become so much more aware of the secret ingredient in my life—intuition.

I believe that we are all part of the spiritual world, it doesn't matter which part. I happen to love witches (especially Glinda, the good witch of the north, from my favourite movie of all time, *The Wizard of Oz*). Learning how to interpret the meanings of this spiritual world has brought another level to my own journey. I have loved finding out more about myself as well as how our energies can heal ourselves and others. These other-worldly practices have been a great way to recognise my own abilities, shape my creativity, build imagination and improve my self-confidence.

I also am a fan of angel cards (my deck has the most gorgeous pictures on them). My set of fairy tarot cards is a 78 card deck full of vintage-style illustrations that depict the old world of Glastonbury in Somerset, England (another reason I love them). The fairies depicted on the cards are utterly gorgeous and childlike, just like you would imagine them to be from fairy stories (or from the bottom of the garden, as my grandmother used to say). Fairies are beautiful; they are nature's own angels.

≈ ≈ ≈

For centuries tarot and intuition-based work has had a secretive element about it, but today, it's embraced in many parts of the world. Like traditional tarot cards, there are major cards and minor cards. The first 22 cards are from the major arcana and are numbered; they represent major events and turning points in our lives. I don't seem to pick these ones as much—maybe I am not in that phase of my life right now! The cards for the minor arcana (representing everyday life) consist of four suits, Spring (Wands and the Fire element), Summer (Cups and the Water element), Autumn (Pentacles/Coins and the Earth element) and Winter (Swords and the Air element). Angel cards differ from tarot cards (they don't have those spooky death cards for a start) but instead have messages of encouragement, positivity and optimism, and they don't predict the future. They reflect what is going on in your life right now. You can talk to your own angel. Yes, my friends we all have one (or two): it isn't some magical power that is bestowed upon a few, we all have the power (I'm sure my angels sometimes wish I would shut up).

I like to think of my angel cards as a tool to help my personal development and self-discovery. I ask the question of myself (and this can be anything really, sometimes it's just "What do I need to know today?") and use the cards to help find answers. It's really fun and I look forward to 'speaking' with the fairies every night. I decide how to interpret the cards when they fall; sometimes I take what it says on board and sometimes totally ignore it and choose other cards. There's no right or wrong with the cards, that's what makes it fun! Angel cards give cues or clues about something or someone in my life that I am either hesitant about, or haven't quite accepted, or I just find myself standing at a crossroad and I don't know what direction to go (it happens). The cards allow me to use my own initiative to make decisions about my life.

Being truly able to embrace this new thought process and gain insight into the 'why' has made my life full of potential. These practices support me in my life's journey with messages of assurance and belief in myself. It has given me a greater understanding of how I can use these new-found skills to enrich my daily life and tap into even more worldly witchy poo wisdom.

Love Actually

"Protect your heart, not from other people but from yourself".

Love is pretty powerful. To have love in your heart is indeed heart warming (I promise I won't get all squishy on you). Love comes when we least expect it; if we go looking for love, it never comes. Love is not something that lives outside of us, love happens for us not to us.

In our day-to-day crazily hectic lives we forget about love. Switch on your radio and you will find that practically every song is about love (or lack of!). Some of my favourite love songs are from the 80s (ha ha!) and one that comes to mind is *'Is this love?'* by Whitesnake (an oldie but a goody!) They question if what they are feeling is love or a dream, and decide it must be love because of its intensity.

When we feel love, our needs are met, we feel loved and cared for and we love ourselves. To love and be loved is what we all want. Love allows us to develop greater compassion for others and connect with those around us.

In Traditional Chinese Medicine (TCM) the heart is where it all starts and ends. The heart is often called 'the house of the mind' as they are intrinsically connected. TCM is about balance and flow, and to lead a heathy emotional life you need to have a happy heart. Joy is the positive emotion of the heart and we need it every day. TCM shows us that the heart stores the Shen, otherwise known as spirit. Love can certainly wrap us up in its warm hug; love and a happy heart are crucial to our quality of life. Our lives rely on the connection with our fellow human beings, our furry friends and the wonderful natural world around us: without it we feel alone and isolated. Caring for ourselves and others allows our heart to be full, and we open ourselves to give and receive love more freely. We feel more open and connected to the world around us and develop greater levels of kind-heartedness. Our heart is the centre of our being and the door to our own happiness. Love lets us focus on what is positive in our lives (oops, I said I wasn't going to get all mushy).

Sometimes when this heart energy is out of balance the opposite is often true. We can overcompensate for a lack of flow to our heart by exhibiting behaviour that is erratic and inappropriate, develop high blood pressure and sometimes even heart attacks! I know what it's like to have a broken heart; it's not always love for another person, it's love for yourself.

I had fallen out of love with myself in the early days of my diagnosis, I really didn't love myself at all. I couldn't see the good in anything that was happening to me. I had all but forgotten what it was like to love myself and to love the things around me.

When we talk about what we don't love—and this can be a myriad of daily events including the traffic, the cold weather, interest rate hikes, parking tickets etc.—we are not focusing on what we do love. We all have the choice to love the things that give us joy, but instead we focus on the negative. I am guilty of this too.

Until recently, I didn't get the connection with feeling happy and saying you're happy. Feeling happy is different because you actually 'feel' it. When I am happy I feel like I could climb Everest,

I'm invincible. I want to harness that every day for the rest of my life because I love that feeling.

When I talk about what I love I feel cheery and I understand the joy it brings and the positive outcomes it has to my life. This is not rocket science; we all know that if we think and talk about what we love, we feel better, we look at life differently, we are healthier and life is good.

When I feel good, I look for things that I love, it's almost a default position now. On my morning walks I see so many things that I love—flowers, animals, houses, trees, the sun, birds and clouds. These things have always been there, but I see them now and realise how much I love having them in my life.

This love-thought practice was instrumental to my recovery. I chose to focus on what I loved in my life rather than what I didn't love. Thinking about what I loved made me feel better, and the better I felt the better my life got. I still had to front up to the hospital every week but I had a smile on my face instead of despair. I remember one of the staff saying on my last day in the oncology ward, "We will miss your smiley face". Wow, that was the biggest compliment anyone could have ever given me. I had been through the toughest challenge of my life and I was smiling and I could feel it. I was starting to love myself again. As time went on I loved going to the hospital, in fact, I couldn't wait until I was there again.

≈ ≈ ≈

I must admit here that some of my favourite movies are from the *Fast & Furious* franchise. I know, it's not the usual roll call of films for the fifty-something mum, but I have seen them all (several times) and it's not the fast cars, the Robin Hood story lines or the beefy actors: it's the significance of family, friendship and love. The main hero in the movie often reflects on his own la famiglia when he reminisces about his father at their family BBQs on Sundays after church. It seems a long way from screeching around the streets in souped-up cars and robbing the rich, but this part of the movie is what I love about it. It doesn't matter what is going on (and there are lot of shenanigans), it's about coming together as family and that doesn't just mean relatives—it's friends (and even past enemies if I recall), anyone who has shown trust, honesty and love. Who would have thought that a tough guy who has spent time in prison could be the central point of domestic bliss?

Yes, sometimes the films are a bit cheesy (and those stunts are amazing but totally unbelievable). I think you either love or hate the *Fast* franchise but I happen to think there are more messages in those films than just triumphs over the criminals, drug lords and obnoxious thieves; there are storylines of sisters, fathers, boyfriends, girlfriends and mates. What's not to love about that? and throw in some very fancy cars and you have a ripping good movie.

No matter what has happened in our lives, we all have the ability to open our hearts to love. Our heart is the centre of our being, it keeps us alive and it rules universal love, balance, empathy and inner peace. When I opened my heart to family, friends, animals and the universe I opened myself up to my creative soul and became more inspired to be a better version of myself.

Big or small, love actually does make the world go round.

Balancing act

Whoa, we're not talking about the highwire here! Yikes, that is scary stuff! A balanced life is a harmonious life. It allows us time to do the things that we love (and time to do those pesky little chores, ho hum). A balanced life feels good; it's the place we want to be. So what happens when we don't have balance in our lives? We feel a bit shizzle, that's what. Our lives need to have equal parts of work and play; when it's lopsided we feel unbalanced.

In fact, studies say that multitasking isn't all that it is cracked up to be. Women are skilled at multitasking (sorry men, it has been scientifically proved) but all that juggling may not be in our best interest. Apparently when we do complex tasks we have to use both sides of our brain, and when we are constantly changing between the two hemispheres, it actually slows us down. We make more mistakes than if we did one thing at a time. This becomes even more of a problem in our fast paced world where distractions happen often (cue Facebook updates!). These distractions can add even more time to the task at hand rather than the other way around.

I was one of those people that thought I was so marvellous because I could do ten things at once. This was an illusion of course, because all I did was make myself more stressed (I see that now!). Being diagnosed with cancer automatically made me slow down. Besides, who wants to be cooking dinner, putting a load of washing on, feeding the dog and talking to your mum on the phone at the same time?

The best way to tackle your day is to consider it in chunks. Some things take no time at all, some need a focus of sixty to ninety minutes. (My oldest daughter has told me on numerous occasions that ninety minutes is the maximum anyone's brain can pay attention, but she was at the time quite frustrated by three hour exams!).

Taking a brain break is important; this is when doing the things we enjoy is crucial. I am definitely a fan of this. Anything that doesn't require us to do or think too much is preferable. Something like taking your dog for a walk or catching up with a friend are great ways to restore balance in your brain so that the next task doesn't overwhelm you. It also gives your brain some space to kick start new thinking patterns.

Exercise

Finding your Balance

Think about what you do on a typical day. How many of those things do you enjoy and how many do you consider to be a duty or chore? Make a list. If you have too many on the 'chore' list then life, my friends, is unbalanced and you're not making enough time to do the things that you love.

Draw up a chart (handwritten is totally fine) and put in a day in your life, write next to each of the hours what you do. Say it goes something like this (this is my day BTW).

10pm – 7am	Sleep (yay, my favourite pastime)
7.am – 7.02am	Take flower essence and aloe vera and write in gratitude journal (2 mins, my friends, to set up your day)
7.02am – 8.30am	Breakfast, shower, a few household chores (ho hum)
8.30am – 9.30am	Take my dog Raffy for a walk
9.30am – 12pm	Work (writing this kinda thing)
12pm – 1pm	Lunch and household chores (ho hum again)
1pm – 4pm	Work (more of writing this kinda thing)
4pm – 6.30pm	I set these hours aside for running children around, visiting family or doing grocery shopping, all those things that have to be done at some point!
6.30pm – 7.15pm	Making dinner (and my family eating it)
7.15pm – 8.15pm	Yoga
8.15pm – 10pm	Sitting on my bum in front of the TV (LOL!)

"*But what about work? I work 10 hours a day, I have no time*", I hear you say. **You have to make time for yourself,** make it a priority to do the things that give you joy. That may mean waking up earlier, that may mean leaving the office earlier so you can take that walk in the park or go swimming.

Make the time. We all have the same amount of time in the day, make each minute count.

Your work should be part of the list that says thumbs up to enjoyment; if you consider work as a chore, that is exactly what it will be.

Change your thought patterns, even if you cannot change your job right now, make a new set of goals to help you reach the life that you are seeking, the life of your dreams.

≈ ≈ ≈

The one thing I hear the most in my daily life (from friends, family and strangers in the supermarket) is "I don't have enough time".

Yet really, we have nothing but time. We actually have all the time in the world, we choose how we want to spend it. My philosophy is that if you have time to complain, moan, watch Netflix and check your social media statuses then you have time to mediate, write in a journal, do yoga and make a list of things that will make your life better. Why wouldn't you want to spend time on all of the things that give you pleasure? All it takes is one decision, no one but you can decide that.

≈ ≈ ≈

You often hear people say "today is a new day" and yes, that is true, but how do you stop yourself from re-living all the past days and make a fresh start, every day? I'm here to tell you that the one thing that has kept my days 'fresh' are daily rituals (and I'm not talking about dancing around a fire or chanting here).

Daily rituals needn't be fancy, nor numerous. Rituals are a great way to help ground you. They are intentional actions you choose to incorporate into your day because they improve your life and how you feel. By definition a ritual is something that we do as a sequence.

My yoga teacher recently said to me that I was very disciplined. I was surprised by this, because I don't consider myself particularly self-controlled. (I really am the queen of being distracted!) When I thought about it, I realised this is what has changed. My life has more order. Not orderly like the army but I have taught myself a system of rules (if you like) to organise my thoughts, behaviours and actions. This is why rituals are so important. Rituals have transformed my everyday tasks into something more meaningful, something that is worthwhile; they have allowed me to pause and reflect on the things that mean something more than just the routine of everyday life. By adopting the practice of rituals I have filled in the gaps that were missing for me to create balance and stability.

I have learned a lot about rituals in my yoga practice. I've been to a few workshops and still find it fascinating that we can adopt something so easy into our lives, something that makes such a massive difference. Rituals differ from habits: habits are actions or behaviours that become automatic; rituals are actions that have a more profound purpose.

I find rituals to be comforting; it's not by accident that our parents incorporated rituals into our lives as children. It gave us the sense of safety in surroundings that may not be familiar or as a wind down to the day. My family still have daily rituals that they practise today that stem from when they were very young. Tuning into what makes sense to us and what brings us stability is paramount for us to feel that we are connected.

I like the philosophies of Ayurvedic medicine, one of the world's oldest healing systems. Ayurveda is the sister science to yoga and was developed in India thousands of years ago. It's based on the belief that health and wellness depend on the balance between mind, body and spirit. Ayurveda is based on the principles of three primary doshas (or energies) known as Vata, Pitta and Kapha. Each of us has a proportion of these three energies that shape our character and personality, from our hair colour, body structure, looks, behaviours, voice, sleep patterns, favourite foods etc.

There is always a predominate dosha that establishes your individual disposition; online quizzes can help you determine your very own dosha (if you don't know it). I am Pitta, and there is no denying that. The characteristics of a Pitta dosha are fair skin that burns easily, light or red hair, always warm or hot (that's me, sweaty betty city) inflamed skin, heartburn, freckles, perfectionism and irritability (to name a few). When doshas become aggravated or out of balance, our bodies and minds can become overwhelmed and out of balance. For example, when I get frustrated or irritable, I get red patches of skin on my face. I can feel it (and see it) straight away; this is my body's way of saying, 'Keep it cool Jane'. And not surprisingly, the worst foods I can eat are peppers, chilli, hot spicy food, oily and fried foods. Strangely (or not) I don't like these foods, I think my body knows that already. I also need to stay away from Bikram Yoga, saunas and any hot steamy environments, which would explain why I find it very unsettling in climates like Bali. It's all very fascinating. Even before I did the dosha test, I knew I was a Pitta: it kind of explained a lot. To balance my dosha I rely on daily rituals to create balance, peace and discipline.

There are literally thousands of rituals, some you will already be doing and not know it! It's actually not that hard, especially once you get into the swing of things.

There's something quite lovely about self-care rituals; it's a chance to do something for you, a gift of sorts every day. I am a fan. What's all this I hear you say? "How can I fit more into my day? I'm too busy".

My daily rituals take less than 2 minutes, yes, 2 minutes a day... That's it.

Exercise

Establishing your Rituals

These are my morning rituals:

When I get out of bed every day, I put my feet on the floor and say *"Thank you for the awesome day I am going to have".*

I take 7 drops of flower essence.

I take 30 ml of aloe vera juice.

I write 3 things that I am grateful for (and sometimes this can just be that I'm grateful nothing has fallen off now that I'm fifty! LOL).

I encourage you to adopt some of these ideas for your daily rituals (start off with at least three).

- Enjoy a hot lemon or ginger drink before breakfast (treat yourself to a gorgeous new cup).
- Take a long walk in nature (so much easier if you have a furry friend).
- Bring fresh flowers into your home.
- Journal your day, take some time out to write about all the good things that have happened in your day.
- Play one of your favourite songs.
- Cloud and stargaze, a form of mediation that I love; there's nothing better than lying on the grass and watching the clouds float by.

Once you have found the rituals that really resonate with you, adopt them into your every day. It's a gift that keeps on giving.

The Thief of Joy

Have you ever wanted to buy bright red flowery pants and then stopped yourself because you thought 'What will people think? I'll look foolish'? Well I am here today to say to you "Who cares?" Dare to be different. Other people's lives are not better, bigger, brighter, wealthier or happier than yours. Buy the pants!

I recently read something that advises not to fight the real you. I love that. Embracing what you are born with is a great safeguard against life's many challenges. We are all different—that's the wonderful thing about being human—we are unique in every way. It doesn't matter what anyone else thinks, does or sees. You are you. Constantly thinking and comparing ourselves to others is fruitless. We judge ourselves against others without realising that our own happiness is more important. We need to let go of the tendency to compare ourselves to others and live our lives—not theirs.

In our fast-paced world of social media it's impossible not to be confronted with images of people's lives every day and compare ours to theirs. I know it's hard when you see people holidaying in the Maldives (who wouldn't want to go there!) but gauging our own self-worth against others can lead to unhappiness and low self-worth because we think we're not good enough. We rarely congratulate ourselves and applaud our achievements. Every one of us does wonderful things every day; we are too hard on ourselves. If only we could embrace and engage the tools we have already have within, we wouldn't need to go searching another person's life and think that theirs is better than ours.

There is no such thing as 'normal'. Chasing another person's idea of life is not living the gift that you have—your own life. I love the Kermit the Frog song *It's not easy being green*; it's one of my favourite childhood songs. He sings about not fitting in, about wanting to be flashy, but by the end of the song he's happy being ordinary.

Ordinariness is pretty special too I think. I am fascinated by the ordinary. People just going about their business, regardless of what that is. To many it may be mundane, pedestrian, even boring. They may be unremarkable, they may be unexceptional, but I happen to love that. Every one of us has a story to tell; I happen to think that the ordinary is in fact, extraordinary. I agree with Kermit—I'm green, and that's awesome.

What makes us so beautiful inside and out is our inner self, the one that is truly you. Each day we have the opportunity to become better at being ourselves and celebrating the life we have. There is no one else like you, and only you can live your life the way you desire. Respect yourself for the life path you have chosen, trust your instincts and replace comparison with self-love.

I hazard a guess that partly the reason that I don't give a crap so much anymore is that I recently turned fifty. I have grown especially capable of sniffing out bullshit these days.

So, for fun, here are 50 things that I know now I'm 50:
1. The best is yet to come.
2. You are never too old and it is never too late to do *ANYTHING*.
3. Forget the drama (and let it go, let it goooo).
4. Use that fine crockery in your cupboard (the one you have been

waiting for a special occasion, *TODAY* is a special occasion).
5. Spend time with people you love and make you feel happy (if they don't, then spend a lot less time with them).
6. Shop in charity shops (the ultimate in recycling).
7. You really can't party like you used to (I know, bummer, but it's true).
8. Every day is a gift.
9. Do something for yourself *TODAY*.
10. It's OK to stay in your dog-walking clothes all day.
11. Living a grateful life is worth it.
12. Wearing no make-up is empowering.
13. We all make mistakes.
14. Yoga has been the best find of my life.
15. Choosing happiness is a choice.
16. However bad a situation may be, you *WILL* get through it.
17. Live in the now (it's all we really have).
18. Failures are all lessons.
19. Make yourself priority number #1, always.
20. I have a lot left to learn.
21. What other people think is none of my business (AKA stop worrying about what other people think of you).
22. Get over yourself (and stop taking yourself too seriously).
23. Downtime is not a waste of time.
24. No parent is perfect.
25. Say no (and don't waste any time thinking about it).
26. Your heath is your wealth (mammograms and colonoscopies are now par for the course).
27. Menopause is shizzle.
28. I'm loving myself more (for being exactly who I am).
29. Having long hair in your 50s is totally acceptable.
30. Listen to what your mum says about your ancestry.
31. Dare to be different.

32. I can now get cheaper insurance.
33. Speak up, it's OK to say how you feel.
34. Stop having negative thoughts about aging; rejoice.
35. Learn something new (often).
36. Take probiotics (your tummy will love you).
37. Don't settle for anything less than your contentment.
38. De-cluttering is uplifting (I should do it more often).
39. Stop watching the news (it's totally depressing).
40. Going to bed early has wonderful benefits.
41. It doesn't matter if your home isn't always clean and tidy.
42. A best friend never goes out of fashion.
43. Sensible shoes are sensible.
44. Stop at amber lights.
45. Embracing change is scary but doable.
46. Face your fear (whatever it is).
47. Ask for help (there is always someone there for you).
48. Spending time with yourself is paramount.
49. Learn something new every day (no matter how small or big).
50. Ride the rollercoaster of life, those up and downs are the best parts.

Cheerleaders

A cheerleader is defined as *"an enthusiastic and vocal supporter of someone or something"*. Why would we not want to surround ourselves with people that uplift and support us?

We make partnerships, friendships and acquaintances throughout our life; sometimes these people are for life and some are fair-weather. I am the person I am today because of the friendships and partnerships I've forged over my fifty years. At each stage of my life people have come and gone for many different reasons, whether that was to teach me something, or to help me understand something about myself, or just a friendship for fun. The ones that have had the biggest impact on me are the people who are still in my life today and have stayed by my side through thick and thin. They are my true soul family. Sometimes what you think is your true partnership in life is not always the most obvious.

Jo is my best friend, I've known her for 16 years and she is my go-to gal for everything and anything. We can while away the hours talking about life challenges, relationships, travel, tarot cards, parenting or just reminiscing about our favourite eighties music. We speak to each other every day, without fail. She sometimes sends me quotes, article links or just the goings on in her life. She tells me what I need to hear (whether I want to hear it or not!) and she is so wise, full of self-esteem and hilariously funny. I admire and respect her and her judgment. I have learnt so many wonderful lessons from her; she is one of my true partners in life.

The other is my husband. We met when I was twenty years old, which makes us now partners of over thirty years, almost unheard of these days. People ask me what the secret is. Well I happen to think there isn't one; he is part of my soul family. God knows we have been through the mill in our thirty years; it hasn't always been easy, far from it! But he too has taught me how to be patient and helped me navigate the ups and downs of life. He has stood by me through illness, sorrow and elation. He knows what's right and wrong and he has an unbelievable ability to see things in everyday life that are (mostly) invisible to me. I walk around with my head in clouds; he is strongly attached to terra firma. We aren't total opposites; although they say that opposite attract I happen to think that you have to have some similarities in the way you look at the world and share common ground on some things, parenting for instance!

Friendships can be complicated, especially as an adult. This is an overhang of our days in the schoolyard when we essentially made friends by just asking someone if we 'could' be friends. This doesn't happen when you get older. Letting people into our inner sanctum is getting harder in the social media world where we are more connected to people at the swipe of a button. Developing and maintaining friendships in this digital age is even more important than ever. Being face to face with another person is still a huge part of what makes us human. Being in the physical presence of someone is paramount to making connections with other people.

Throughout my years of friendships and partnerships, I have learnt a lot about what makes an enriching relationship and what doesn't. I've learnt some pretty amazing lessons from many people and I believe in turn I have helped other people through their own challenges. I'm a bit of a 'go-to person' when it comes to navigating difficult situations, and I like the fact that people think of me that way. I value my friendships. The strong bonds I have with many of my friends is a testament to them as much as to me. If a relationship is important to me, I will make all the effort I possibly can.

I believe that the people we want to hang around have characteristics we don't have (or see) in ourselves. Our friends should complement us, bring out the best in us and be brave enough to tell us when we have spinach in our teeth. My friends are my backbone, they support me and inspire me to be the best version of myself. I feel blessed every day to have such wonderful people in my life, they keep me laughing when times are tough. Sometimes when I am waiting for a friend to arrive and I see them in a distance approaching the coffee shop or restaurant, I get a burst of joy, I am so excited to see them and hear all about what's been going on in their lives. I feel like a child on Christmas morning—the anticipation is just the same. Spending a few hours reminiscing, chatting, laughing and catching up is my one of my favourite ways to spend a morning or afternoon. Friendship to me is about belonging, sharing and being part of something.

The people you spend the most time with are your 'team'. Make sure that you surround yourself with people who share the same life goals as you. If you don't, your team will end up harming you, not helping you. Take a leaf out of the cheerleaders' book: they are a team (there's no 'i' in team), they rely on each other, they support each other (in those eye watering pyramids) and they praise each other for a job well done.

Get the right cheerleading team behind you.

≈ ≈ ≈

Everyone has a place and purpose in our lives but we need to recognise when the relationship has come to its natural end. This isn't easy either; we continue to see people that we know are not good for us for fear that we will upset them. The truth is, these are the people that we need to let go of the most. If you associate with people who are negative, self-absorbed and lazy, they will bring you down with them. You will by osmosis become just like them. It's a hard lesson to learn. I call these people energy drainers, and I'm sure you know a few. They are always moaning and the world is always out to get them. They are misery on wheels. Who wants to spend time with those types of people? Not me. I have become very aware of these types of people and I give them a wide berth now. Their principles don't sit well with me and I question why they have to be so critical of everything when they have so many reasons to be positive and grateful and to celebrate their lives.

I find myself these days listening to people's conversation (eavesdropping I know!) and I am mostly dismayed at the amount of negativity I hear people saying about others. I will own up here too, I am not immune from this either but I have in recent years been very mindful of not speaking poorly about anyone or anything. If I find myself doing it, I backtrack and start the conversation again. Being derogatory or critical of other people just makes me feel bad—it says more about me than it does about the person in question. This has been something I have worked on a lot; I refuse to get into any conversations now that may lead to disparaging comments.

This hasn't been easy, because in the past I have been one to gossip and make someone out to be worse than they are. I don't want to be that person anymore, that person sucks. I feel embarrassed now that I used to speak about others with disdain. I would be mortified if someone spoke about me that way, but that's what I was doing, so that had to stop. How could I be a generous, kind and forgiving person if behind the scenes I was gossiping and being nasty? I had to own up to that and decide to be a better person and respect others and their decisions. This sounds easy on paper but when I realised just how much I was complaining and gossiping, I made it my mission to be aware of my thoughts and the people around me who were feeding the negativity. I know it isn't possible to totally desert some people in your life, but recognising that they are not good for you is the first step, then make a conscious effort to spend less and less time with them. Give yourself time away from them and start to make new friends, friends that encourage, inspire and motivate you.

I know it's difficult to not take on other people's negative opinions, thoughts and feelings; it seems to ooze from their aura into the atmosphere around us. I try not to let these external influences affect my daily life; when people around me are being all Negative Nancy I say to myself, "I cannot control others, only myself". And this has helped enormously.

Embrace the Weird
(and wonderful you)

Nowadays, my children often say to me, "Mum, can you stop being weird". "Hmm", I say to them, "I'm not being weird, I'm being me and I will never stop being me. What exactly is weird anyway?" In my children's dictionary it means 'stop being *NOT* normal'. Why is it that we find it hard to express our real selves? I love joking around, dancing silly steps around the family room, pulling faces and generally being a big kid. It is joyful, and makes me laugh. Why do we stop doing these things when we become adults? Do you recall being admonished that with adulthood comes both responsibility and the knowledge of how to use it wisely? This sounds more like the fun police to me. It's like a switch has been turned off when your eighteenth birthday comes around, the 'no more fun for you' switch. Yes, becoming an adult is part of life and there are responsibilities—but there is also fun, life should be fun. Isn't that the point?

When I trekked Tuscany in 2017 (with nineteen other women who had had their own cancer experiences), we visited the gorgeous town of Lucca. Within a few hours of arriving we found a carousel, the old fashioned type, with dancing horses, wild animals, garlands and streamers. Without even thinking twice four of us stood in the queue waiting to buy tickets. We all jumped at the chance to be foolish, to be childlike and to have fun. We didn't care that we were the only ones on it, just us, the crazy Australian women who were squealing with delight, riding around and around on the carousel. We had such a fun day. I felt like a child again. There's something to be said for that wondrous feeling of the wind in your hair as you whirl around on your chosen horse. I couldn't take the smile off my face. In fact when I visited the following year, I went on it again and I have since made a bee-line for many other carousels around the world, much to my children's disdain, "There goes Mum again".

I am endlessly fascinated by people who don't give a shizzle and live life to its fullest. Their glass is always half full, never empty. I love seeing people who live their life on their own terms and are their true selves. I admire them and am in awe of the fact that they know who they are and don't pretend to be anyone else but themselves. This is something that I am still working on; I think that we all put masks on from time to time. We don't want the world to see the real us—I certainly put a mask on when I was first diagnosed with breast cancer. I didn't want anyone to know. I just carried on with life like nothing had happened; the status quo was better than what was actually happening. Because I wasn't the type of person to upset the apple cart (I am a Libran after all), I hid behind a made up version of myself because I was embarrassed that my life wasn't that fantastic after all. I had spent so many years creating a façade I couldn't possibly face the fact that my life wasn't all that it was cracked up to be.

If there's anything I regret in my life, it's that I became too caught up in what people thought of me. I felt that I had to conform just like many other people had, at the expense of what my inner self was actually telling me. This is mostly true about my career; if I think about it, I was always creative, I used to draw, read and write and I was fascinated by flowers and plants as a child. If I had listened to my own heart, I would have pursued a career in something very different and I wouldn't have cared whether anyone thought that was a good idea or not. I don't feel that's a selfish thing at all.

I missed a massive opportunity to be the real me, and it's taken a long time to get back to that place of peace about who I actually am. I conformed to society's beliefs about what was a 'real' job and promptly set about forging a corporate career, in spite of the fact that my intuition was telling me otherwise. This was partly from my upbringing, but partly because it was what all my friends were doing—it was the eighties after all. The era of 'greed is good' and possibly the start of this current notion of success that is intrinsically tied to money and power. I was swept along like many others at the time but found myself thirty years later thinking, 'Is this the life I had dreamed of?' No, is the answer.

When I was growing up my mum had quite a few university friends who I thought were so groovy (yeah, it was the seventies), they wore kaftans, flowery shirts and platform sandals. They lived in mud brick homes, raised chickens and grew broad beans. I even think some of them were painters and sculptors, definitely the artsy type. I have such fond memories of visiting them; life was simple, uncomplicated, fun and they just seemed to be having a ball. I don't know whether they were or not (I hope so) but those images have stuck in my mind, because part of me has always wanted to emulate that life. The carefree, creative life they had was something that appealed to me enormously.

I grew up in country Victoria, where the summers were boiling hot and the winters could freeze your buns off. The days were enormously long for a child, full of promise of seeing friends, riding bikes and submerging yourself in endless H_2O. Life was simple and straightforward. My mum's broad bean eating friends were no exception; I can remember countless summers swimming in rivers near their homes. They weren't weird, that was life in the country, life as they knew it, and life where you could be yourself, no one cared. I don't know if that is a seventies thing when life was less complicated or whether they really didn't give a crap. I sense the later.

When I reminisce about my younger years, I come over all a bit melancholy. I don't wish to live in the town I grew up in but I wish for a simpler life. And I wish that we could all live a life where we could be ourselves and not a version of that—a version of what other people think life should be. I feel that if I was left to my own devices I would be wearing a kaftan and writing books in a mud brick home! I'm sure my children would have something to say about that...

Funny how life can do a full circle, mine has. That imaginative little girl has come back to her creative life like a homing pigeon—it just took thirty years! Hey, there's no time like the present. So I say, be you, who cares what other people think, no one cares, and quite frankly who cares if they do. Embrace all the crazy things that make you happy; it's not weird, or odd or even bizarre, it's you. So if you want to design homes, wear sequinned shoes or start learning the salsa, then do it. Express that inner part of you that just wants to have fun and stay true to the person you are, and don't take yourself too seriously. Start where you mean to finish. If your awesome personality shines, so will the life around you. It's universal law; make your day and someone else's will also glow that little bit brighter.

I want to tell you a story here, because I love it (and I love my girlfriend). She had (later in life) qualified to be a nurse. She had up until that time been a dance teacher and her life was always filled with sparkles and glitter. On her very first day as a qualified nurse, she got ready in her uniform and looked in the mirror. She had purple streaks in her hair, a pink ribbon attached to her ponytail, a name tag that had hearts all over it and a fob watch that was attached with a sequinned bow. She started as she meant to finish. She didn't care what anyone else thought, and I can tell you that the patients love her.

Call to adventure

By definition, wanderlust means *"a strong desire to travel"*. For me this translates to "obsessive need to travel".

I love travelling: it's all I have ever wanted to do, I spend all my savings on it, I dream about it, I plan it and I budget for it. Travel is my world, being able to explore this magnificent planet is a gift, and one that is available to all of us. It doesn't matter where you go. You can go twenty kilometres up the road and experience something new, something magical, meet new people and infuse yourself in a different everyday living. And as a bonus, you come back more knowledgeable, happier and more suntanned (possibly).

Travel to me is a meaningful pursuit, a time to look beyond what's in front of my face; it's my place to learn. As a child I would read musty dog-eared textbooks in geography lessons and gaze in wonderment at all of these exotic sounding countries and famous monuments and try to imagine what it must be like to visit them.

It seemed a pipedream, a fantasy, something that you aspired to do when you were a grown-up. But when you actually do it, you have to pinch yourself; you cannot actually believe that you are standing in front of the Eiffel Tower or the Tower Bridge or walking the cobblestones of Rome. You are that child again gazing in amazement and wonder.

So you may be wondering now, how does travelling uncomplicate your life?

Some people may think that it makes life more complicated! and yes, sometimes it does but for me, there is nothing like travel to lift the spirits, it was just the tonic to get me back on track after my life came apart at the seams.

Even when I was having weekly chemotherapy I thought about travelling and in fact I did. It was my way of normalising what was happening, it was my comfort zone and I didn't want what was happening around me to impact my love of travelling. I can't say that my specialists were all for the idea, they were hesitant to be suggesting that I left the shores only weeks after treatment had ended, but I didn't care. Some may think I was foolish to put my health in jeopardy (I know my Mum did) but it was my way of coping, to do something as ordinary and routine as travel was my saviour. I spent three weeks in America only a month after I finished radiotherapy. My specialist armed me with a bagful of medication (just in case, which I didn't use thankfully) and it was the first time I had ever left our shores without full travel insurance because they wouldn't cover me. I was also still coping with second degree burns from my treatment but I was not going to let anything stop me.

Travel is, and always will be, my go-to when the chips are down, in fact, many of my holidays have been when I could least afford it, health wise or financially. Those are also my favourites; there's something about having nothing that makes the experience all that more extraordinary. That's not to say I haven't had moments of counting all of that shrapnel in the bottom of my purse to buy a train ticket or burn lotion from the nearest pharmacy.

When we travel we interact with new cultures, things, people, landscapes and different ways of living. Moving away from what we know and our daily routines allows us to get in touch with what truly inspires us.

Being in contact with people of different cultures helps us to appreciate and accept our differences. We learn new ways of thinking and I believe this makes us more open minded, tolerant and objective.

I like to call travel "the mind retreat". In our busy lives, a getaway can recharge our brain batteries and give us the break we all need. Travel is one of the very best ways for me to reset, recharge and detox from the everyday stresses that I enviably encounter.

Travel is freedom, freedom to explore and freedom to be the person that no one knows. I cannot recommend it highly enough; I get all jittery when I even think about where I can travel to next. I have certainly travelled a lot, and whilst I wouldn't recommend all the destinations I have visited, there are plenty that have been perfect. I am constantly on the move, even if some of that time is in my head! As soon as I return from one holiday, I am booking the next, I can't help myself. To look forward to a holiday is the best part. I'm guilty of scanning accommodation and tourist information websites for hours on end (when I should actually be doing something else).

I could tell you a hundred travel stories (I won't here!) but let me share one with you about why I love travelling so much. There is mystery, fascination and mishaps to every travel adventure whether that be the ordinary, the local or the dream location, it doesn't matter where. It's often who you are with and what you are experiencing that makes travelling so special. Let me tell you about my big sister.

When I was contemplating trekking Tuscany again I emailed my sister with all the details in anticipation that she may want to join me. I wasn't confident that she would consider flying in a steel tube half way across the world to walk 100 kilometres through the Italian countryside. She had never travelled farther than New Zealand in her fifty-two years.

When I received her return email, it would be an understatement to say that I was shocked; I nearly fell off my chair. I had to read it three times before I realised that she had said yes. This was a big deal. My sister had never done a long haul flight, been in a country where they didn't speak English, seen an ancient treasure or travelled in a car that drove on the other side of the road.

The first consideration for a travel novice is the extremely long flight. Without even thinking about it, I booked our flight to Florence straight through, thirty-six hours in transit. Oops.

By the time we arrived in Florence my sister was a paler shade of white, hyperventilating, gagging at the smell of the blocked toilets near the entrance to the airport and announcing loudly that she would never do a long haul flight again. At this time I didn't want to mention that we would be doing it all again to get home.

A quick trip in the taxi (with the windows down) allowed her time to gather herself and before we knew it we were deposited at our rather lovely hotel. We had arrived, phew, I had got her there in one piece (and thankfully she hadn't vomited).

On our first night in Florence I asked her why she had decided to do this trip, and her answer was, "I need to get out of my comfort zone". And that's the part of travel that I love. You are out of your comfort zone, big time.

My sister and I travelled through Italy and Austria for a month in late summer 2018. I could go on and on about what we did (and didn't do) but I think my sister's Top 10 trip highlights will give you a good indication of just how much she enjoyed herself.

1. The trek – walking through Tuscany
2. Travelling with Jane (that's me!)

3. Seeing my son (in Vienna)
4. David... that's the statue of David, it was love at first sight
5. Mutts – of all shapes and sizes
6. The weather
7. Italy – Florence, love, love, love and Venice, so different from anything I have ever seen
8. Getting my hair washed and blow dried in Venice (we had after all just spent 10 days trekking!)
9. Meeting Gina and Kate (fellow trekkers, dinner buddies and top chicks)
10. Italian food – apertivo hour with snacks.

And the best part for me was to see these amazing sights through a fresh pair of eyes. I had visited most of the places previously but to experience it with someone who had never seen such beauty reminds me of just why I travel. The sheer pleasure of seeing, hearing and experiencing how people in other parts of the world live is to connect with our fellow human beings. I am constantly reminded of the generosity of communities, the awe inspiring landscapes and the history of our world when I travel.

I urge you to step out of your comfort zone and experience what this wonderful world has to offer, who knows, you might just find your own slice of heaven.

≈ ≈ ≈

Travel is the best investment we can make in ourselves. Since my diagnosis I have travelled a lot on my own. This was not intentional; I didn't just wake up one day and say to myself "I want to be a solo traveller from now on". I love sharing my experiences with my husband, family and friends but I came to the conclusion that I needed to travel alone because I had to find myself. I know, it sounds clichéd, I wasn't running off to the nearest ashram but I needed some space to understand and 'find' (for want of a better word) myself. I know what you're thinking: 'Did you really need to rush off overseas to find yourself?' Well, no probably not, because I wasn't trying to escape myself, just find out a little bit more of what made me tick. But I did and I'm glad, because this is when I met some of the most gorgeous people I know.

Trekking Tuscany with my fellow breast cancer survivors was and still is one of the highlights of my life. I know, big call, but I needed it at the time. I needed to see that there was life after cancer, that I could do this. That I could accept what had happened and enjoy everything that life has to offer. These women were living proof that life doesn't end because you got cancer; in fact it has only just begun. They weren't wallowing in their own self-pity; they were standing up and being counted and I admired that immensely. I suspect that travelling the Pilgrim Path in Italy gave me more than I will ever know. When I returned from that trip, I was a different person.

A Recipe for Change

Nobody really likes change. It's scary and unpredictable. We like our comfort zones; it makes us feel secure and self-assured. We don't like rocking the boat; most people would think it would be grand if we could float through life without a lot of change. But change is meant to happen to us; sometimes it's little changes, sometimes big, ugly ones. We react differently to each type. Changing my brand of tea or the colour of my socks is a day-to-day example of little changes that we make in our lives, but when we are faced with massive change, our safe and comfortable existence is questioned. In the face of a considerable change we feel disorientated and confused. Unwanted change is the hardest of all. We have no choice but to face it head on. And that takes courage because surrendering to it is painful.

Change is often a trigger point to make us realise that there is more for us to recognise and achieve in our lives. At the time of abrupt change all we can see is our world tumbling down around us and we want to take cover and cry. I know I did. My life-changing event wasn't welcome; I didn't wish for it, dream about it or want it. I hated the changes that were forced upon me. It wasn't fair. If anyone had told me at the time that this change was necessary for me to grow as a person and see myself differently, I'm pretty sure I would have said something rude to them. As far as I was concerned, it was awful. I had built my life around all the things that I thought were right; just like a house, I thought my foundations were strong and that they could weather any storm. And when they started toppling, I thought 'This is it, my house is sinking and I can't save it'.

Let's face it, I don't think the universe want us to live unhappy lives; that's not what the higher powers want for us. I believe that we are all destined to live the life of our dreams but we need to follow the 'recipe for change'. It's not hard, we just forget to add the eggs sometimes and that is what makes it challenging. Sometimes it takes a breakdown to realise that the recipe isn't right or you haven't quite read it properly. If you are anything like me, I read half the recipe and then assume I know the rest. I kinda did the same thing in my life. I was zooming along, not reading the instructions and not taking any notice when the result was flat and unappetising. Until my life was smouldering in the bottom of the oven did I stop to realise that I had not only used the wrong recipe, it was now on fire.

I had to work hard to take myself back to the start and write a new recipe. And I don't mean working 24/7; I mean working hard at believing in myself. Changing my mindset (and my mind state) took some dedication on my part. You don't just wake up one morning with a completely new outlook on life. It takes time to reset the beliefs systems that we've had in place for all those years. It took time for me. And I am still working on it. When I catch myself having negative thoughts or beating myself up, I make sure that I reorganise my thoughts and put a more positive spin on it. It happens all the time actually (I am definitely not immune to feeling shizzle some days even after writing all this!) But I am aware of it and that in itself is a step forward. I worry about things too, about my heath, my finances, all normal things to worry about but I know now that all it takes is changing the way I think and feel about it.

It sounds easy and sometimes it is, and sometimes it's not. But that's my challenge too. Things don't always go my way, sometimes my plans don't work out. But I always stay in the right lane. It takes courage to face up to our disappointments and allow ourselves the space to heal. I have struggled with that too. I forget the enormity of what I've been through and sometimes dismiss that it can take years to fully recover from trauma. I am reminded of this when I visit my GP, who reminds me that I am not wonder woman after all (bummer!)

Embracing change is a blessing in disguise. I see that now but it's hard to fathom at the time. I had to rebuild my house and go back to the very start of the building process. Just like an architect designs a house, I had to redesign my life—that meant a lot of change. But this time, I was looking forward to it; I couldn't wait to get started. Writing this book has been an enormously cathartic exercise for me. It has helped me understand why I felt the way I did, to forgive (mainly myself) and to realise that I am only human and that I make mistakes and I'm not infallible. Change has been a positive experience for me and it has taught me how to be more resilient, stronger and to trust myself. I am not sad I got cancer.

Sometimes the biggest challenges we face are the ones that bring us the greatest good. It seems a crazy thing to say, but I have learned so much from my experience. I would not have done half the things I have done in the past three years if I hadn't had cancer. I would not have twice trekked Tuscany, met gorgeous new friends, started to practise yoga, travelled to Greece two times for a yoga retreat, given up my corporate job or adopted a dog.

Having cancer made me value my life and what was important to me. It made me focus on what really counts, and to forget the rest. I ask myself if it will matter in six months' time; the truth is that nothing is worthy of our worry and no past experience is worthy of us carrying it into our future lives. I now commit to myself and my future; I am the person I was always meant to be. I reward myself; I am constantly learning and redefining my awareness. It's my mission in life—and I choose to accept it!

Just like making a cake, if we leave out an ingredient, the cake doesn't taste (or look) that great. When it comes to making real changes in our life, we can't leave out an ingredient. If you follow the recipe, you will be on the right track. Seeing we are talking about recipes here, I thought I would include one that is super easy, delicious and takes no time at all. (Thanks Sarah!)

Sarah's Fruit & Nut Slice

300 grams almonds
70 grams coconut flakes
70 grams dried cranberries
50 grams pitted dates
3 eggs
3 tablespoons coconut oil

Mix all ingredients in a food processor until it binds.
Empty into a greased baking tray (18 cm x 28 cm)
Bake in a 180°C oven for 20 minutes.
Once cooled spread a handful of sunflower seeds over the top and drizzle with chocolate... YUM!

Yellow Brick Road

Remember in The Wizard of Oz Dorothy was encouraged to follow the yellow brick road? Well today friends, I encourage you too to follow the golden path to the awesome life you deserve. Every single second of the day is an opportunity to change your life because you can change the way you feel. You are always in control of how you feel. It makes no difference what has happened in the past, what mistakes you have made, what you would do differently. None of that matters. What matters is that you can change. Step out into the sunshine.

You only have now, your past was a now, your future will be a now, it's all a now. Being in the now is calming, it has no memory attached to it, and it just is. There's a great comfort in this realisation; enjoy what you have right now, it is perfect. Do not ever waste a minute in regret or disappointment, which is akin to poisoning yourself again. The Greek philosophers had it right; their wisdom is as practical today as it was in ancient times. As Euripides said *"Waste no fresh tears over past griefs."*

It doesn't matter at which point you find yourself on the yellow brick road—you could be just starting your journey—but I assure you that with each passing day you will feel more and more alive. I believe we live in the most exciting times; we have never experienced a world with so much promise. Our world is changing at an amazing speed every day, and our knowledge is growing at a rapid pace too. I cannot tell you how happy I am to be living in this modern world of ours that continues to fascinate me, test me, encourage me and support me in becoming the best version of myself.

≈ ≈ ≈

Who even knows what the future hold for us, but here's the thing—I am more excited about what my life will be than what it has been. I have faith in the future and with all the information available to us now I believe that we can all realise our potential.

We are all capable of wondrous things, we can all be superheros—and not just for one day, but for all of our lives. The most exciting thing is that we actually hold all of those super powers within us, we already have them. Isn't that wonderful? You needn't look any further than yourself, you have the key to unlock your own potential and start living the life you were destined to have.

When we recognise our place in the world we open ourselves up to being present and listening to our surroundings. We don't take enough time out of our busy lives to appreciate the very things right in front of our noses. When we experience awe, we are challenged by the presence of something so much bigger than ourselves. I can totally relate. When I am standing in front of an enormous landscape, watching waves roll into the shore or walking through a field of yellow daffodils, it makes me feel very small in this very large world. It's been said that this feeling connects us to ourselves and each other.

When we see ourselves as part of the whole universe we begin to support the very things that keep our world revolving. We all need to be part of the larger community of earthlings. We need to care and nurture it every day, and whilst we may be only one person in a world of billions, we can make a difference. When we are at one with nature we can live our lives in harmony. In our day-to-day life we forget about these miracles that surround us. Mahatma Gandhi said *"Be the change you want to see in the world"*, and this starts with us.

We cannot always control what goes on in our world but we can start with ourselves. By living a grateful life and appreciating and respecting our fellow human beings we can live by example. We can teach our children to love and nurture themselves and others to create a world of peace. This power is our future. When we stay connected to this feeling of awe, wisdom, prosperity and possibility we are in fact pretty invincible.

I have found my very own emerald city, and all it took was one step. I ultimately now trust in my own abilities, I believe in myself and I have taken charge of my life.

Life is meant to be awesome; it's just taken me a while to work that one out.

"Fear less, hope more; eat less, chew more; whine less, breathe more; talk less, say more; love more, and all good things will be yours".

Swedish proverb

What I Believe
(and things I am currently obsessed with!)

I believe that we are all pretty amazing, each and every one of us. There's no denying that we all face challenges in our lives, but it is how we react to them that makes the difference between a life half lived and a life full of love.

I sprout this a lot around my house and I get my fair share of eye rolling from my family, particularly the teenagers in my life. As a parent I feel compelled to teach my children that they are in charge of their own lives, that they are able to make choices and decisions based solely on living the life they choose and the life they deserve, whatever that may be for them. They get to choose. This doesn't mean they can skirt out of their responsibilities mind you, but I encourage them to really think about the person they are and how they can make an impact on their inner world and the world around them. I believe that we can teach our children to be their best versions of themselves when they practise gratitude, self-love, compassion and mindfulness.

I don't want them to fall into the trap that I did, and not listen to their inner selves. For most of my life I thought I wasn't worthy of pursuing my dreams, that they were fanciful, far-fetched realities and that a creative career was not a proper job. Most people I knew growing up were fearful of life; they worked in jobs they hated, desperately waiting for the weekends and holiday times when they could steal a few hours doing the things that they truly loved. Somehow your 'life' was just a matter of going through the motions and existing only to be afraid of what could possibly happen next. They seemed so consumed with the future and all its possible consequences that they forgot to live. It was like they were so scared of dying that they forgot to live.

If I have learnt anything, it is that we should be filled with enthusiasm every day for what this amazing gift of life has in store for us. This is one of the most important things I can pass on to my children. A life of promise, joy, good health, love and compassion is available to everyone. I want them to follow their dreams and experience an unlimited life, just as it should be.

≈ ≈ ≈

Fast track to fifty and whilst my life has changed a lot, I wouldn't change it for the world. This wonderful thing we call life is a gift—I guess you learn that in half a century. No matter what life throws at us, we are all capable of so much (even though we don't think we are). There is a certain comfort in knowing that all will be well, even in times of change, disappointment, fear and sadness. To travel these paths is the path of life, and the one we are destined to walk. To trust in life, is life itself; that is the ultimate skill my friends.

≈ ≈ ≈

Throughout this inner voyage of mine (I still hate the word journey), I started reading (a lot) and found some awesome books, magazines and websites that really helped me understand not only myself but how to change my life without having to necessarily leave my house. I started to see why gratitude, self-love and well-being are a joyous and rewarding way of life—it wasn't as hokey as I thought!

I have transformed my life into one that I had only dreamt about. I have fulfilled a reality for myself that is beyond what I ever thought I could have achieved.

I am grateful for each of these book resources (and their authors, although I don't personally know them!) that have helped me on my way:

Why People Fail – Siimon Reynolds
The Art of Living – Thich Nhat Hanh
Big Magic – Elizabeth Gilbert
You Can Heal Your Life – Louise Hay
Sane New World – Ruby Wax
Bonkers – Jennifer Saunders
Thrive – Adriana Huffington

As you know, I also started practising yoga. I really didn't like it to begin with, it made me feel nauseous and sick (goodness knows why I kept going back) but it proved to be the shift that I needed and I now cannot even think about my life without yoga, it really did save my life.

I am obsessed now with the little things in life, the things that in the past I took for granted and paid no attention to.

I am also obsessed (in no particular order) with:
- Herbal tea (I honestly have over thirty different flavours in my pantry)
- Decluttering
- Stationery (this is not new!)

- Kombucha
- Fabric softener (especially the violet scented one)
- Patterned Yoga pants
- Moon cycles
- Succulents
- Sleep insights on my FitBit
- Aromatherapy
- Sweet potato chips

Inspiring quotes (these are some of my favourites):
- *There are no mistakes, only lessons.* – Chinese proverb
- *The most important relationship you will ever have is with yourself.* (I wrote that one!)
- *Love is the energy of life.* – Robert Browning
- *Imagination is everything. It is the preview of life's coming attractions.* – Albert Einstein
- *Like attracts like.*
- *If you get stuck, choose another pen.* (I have a few pens now!)
- *Be the person you are looking for.* (Amen to that.)

- Charity shops
- Smiling at people in the street
- Slow cooking
- Shredding (paper that is)
- Dog coats (knitted ones particularly)
- Beanies (especially the ones with pom poms)
- Numerology
- 5 ingredient recipe books

Thank You

I am beyond lucky to have so many people in my life that not only support me in my passion for writing, but offer their help every day to allow me to live my creative life and encourage me to be the best version of myself.

Ray, Imogen and Trinity, my everything, always.

Joanne, my right hand woman (who is left handed), life friend and breakfast buddy.

To my parents, with all my love.

My family, we may be like a patchwork quilt but I love you all.

Susan and Clare at White Space Yoga and Light Space Yoga, your studios are my home away from home.

My sister Natalie, I cannot wait for our next big adventure.

Anna Blatman, your paintings are beautiful and so are you.

The Marilyns (my sisterhood).

My friends, to have you all in my life is a blessing.

Caroline, reflexologist extraordinaire.

Tania, acupuncturist from heaven.

Robern and family, your gingerbread is still my favourite.

Michelle and her team at Accentia Design, thank you, thank you, and thank you.

Desolie, your editing skills are beyond this world.

Annemieke and Jane HJ, spending anytime with you both is a privilege.

Noelene, your enthusiasm for life shines wherever you go.

Louisa, your Magick Mondays are the highlight of my week.

Bernie and Joan, you live in the most extraordinary corner of the world and I cannot wait to come back.

About the Author

JANE DELAHAY

Jane Delahay is a Melbourne based author and dedicated Yogi.

Jane has written two previous books;
'*The Leap Year*' is part memoir about her own breast cancer story and part travel journal about trekking in Tuscany.

'*Four for the Road*' delves into the world of travel writing about a road trip with her husband and teenage children around the UK and Scotland.

Jane is married, with two daughters, one dog and two cats.

www.janedelahay.com

Enjoy more of Jane's writing at:
www.facebook.com/janedelahay.author
www.instagram.com/janedelahay/

www.ingramcontent.com/pod-product-compliance
Lightning Source LLC
Chambersburg PA
CBHW071907290426
44110CB00013B/1306